D1162195

IRISH MONKS IN THE GOLDEN AGE

IRISH MONKS
IN
THE GOLDEN AGE

By Various Writers

Edited by
REV. PROFESSOR JOHN RYAN, S.J.

DUBLIN: CLONMORE AND REYNOLDS LTD.
LONDON: BURNS AND OATES

First Published 1963

MADE AND PRINTED IN THE REPUBLIC OF IRELAND
BY SEALY, BRYERS & WALKER LTD., DUBLIN, FOR
CLONMORE & REYNOLDS LTD.

CONTENTS

Acknowledgement

The Publishers express their thanks to Radio Éireann for permission to print this set of Thomas Davis lectures, broadcast under the title THE IRISH MONKS IN A FALLING WORLD.

I

THE FALLING WORLD

BY REV. PROFESSOR JOHN RYAN, S.J.

Y o u will no doubt have noticed the expression "A Falling World". The term requires some explanation. What exactly was the world which was falling? Why was it falling? What was the extent of the fall: was it from a noble height to a lowly and depressing depth? Were the victims unable to arrest the process of collapse? What were their powers of recuperation when the worst had happened? Let me try to give very brief answers to these questions.

Could we go back to the year 400 we would find Europe very different from what it is to-day. There would be no kingdom of Great Britain, no France, no Belgium, no Holland, no Spain, no Switzerland, no Austria, no Italy, no Portugal as separate and independent states. All that vast area was then part of the Roman Empire. In fact the region I have just mentioned would be no more than a third or perhaps a fourth of the Empire as it then existed, for the Roman boundaries on the east reached to Babylon and to the Caspian Sea and south of the Mediterranean occupied Egypt and the lands bordering the Mediterranean from Egypt to the Straits of Gibraltar. It was an Empire that included the most diverse peoples and races, Britons, Gauls, Iberians, Italians, Greeks, Copts, Jews, Arabs. One great state embraced them all: the nomad shepherds in their black tents beside the Sahara, the camel drivers beside the Tigris and the Euphrates, the fisherfolk on the Atlantic coast, the simple tillers of the soil within sight of the Scottish highlands, the sophisticated citizens of Athens, Alexandria and Rome. And that Empire was no mere conglomeration of disparates which a single shock might dissipate; it had lasted already, despite its unwieldy extent, for some five centuries. It was a unit of civilization. It was, in its own view, *the* civilized world. At its heart stood one sole ruler, the Emperor. Its system of government by state officials, each with its own duties, in every part of the realm, was the most perfect that mankind had till then seen. Its safety was guaranteed by the large, skilfully organized, traditionally-triumphant Roman army. Its citizens, in their relations with one another, were subject to the same law, that Roman Law whose principles of reason, justice and humanity were to pass as a precious legacy to posterity. Its roads, stations, elaborate transport arrangements made travel easy and speedy from Hadrian's Wall in Britain to the borders of Persia. Its weights and measures and coinage were everywhere the same. Its merchants profited by the universal peace to increase the general prosperity. Its public buildings, baths, theatres, bridges, villas, markets were then unique and would be remarkable in any epoch. Its teachers brought to the youth of cities, towns and even the larger villages, the benefits of a first-class education. It is not perhaps surprising that for four hundred years, from the reign of Augustus, the first Emperor, to the time with which we are now dealing, the beginning of the fifth century, the citizens of the Roman Empire regarded themselves as privileged beings. They were content with their lot. No nation within the Empire sought independence in withdrawal; still less did any province or any collection of provinces seek its overthrow. On the contrary, it was the common belief of Roman citizens that the Empire of Rome would last forever. *Roma Aeterna,* Eternal Rome, was no empty phrase but the concise expression of a truth conceived to be axiomatic.

Nor was this view confined to the pagan citizens of the Empire. It was shared in extraordinary fashion by the Christians also. There is no need to stress the fact that the tradition of the Empire was through and through pagan. In the Roman Pantheon the gods were a multitude. Their number went on increasing by the incorporation of deities from the religions of the conquered peoples. But one particular deity all had to accept, the Emperor of the day, who represented the majesty and the glory of the State. All had to join in rendering him divine honours. To fail in this duty was to proclaim oneself a bad citizen. This was the most acute of problems for the early Christians. They refused to offer the official sacrifices to the Emperor as if he were a god and were therefore persecuted. The number of Christians put to death, often with cruel tortures, between the reign of Nero and the end of the reign of Diocletian is reckoned in millions. Nevertheless their loyalty to Rome never faltered. By the end of the third century it was obvious that the efforts of the Emperors to stamp out Christianity were doomed to failure. In 313 Constantine the Great issued the Edict of Milan which put the Christian religion on the same legal footing as the worship of the gods. From that day forward paganism began to recede and Christianity to take its place as the religion of the Roman people. In the Theodosian Code, a bulky collection of the laws of the Empire, completed in 438, the Christian Faith was recognized as the religion of the Roman State. By the year 400, therefore, the union between the Roman Empire and the Christian religion was already intimate. A blow to the State would be regarded by the bishops and the faithful as a blow to the Church as well.

No institution in this world is perfect. It goes without saying that the Roman Empire, for all its size and strength, was exposed to dangers from within and from without. From within came the endemic disease of all mighty organizations, the tendency to proliferate, to add department to department, cell to cell, until the ultimate growth is like a cancer on the body politic. Taxes became oppressive. Citizens wearied of the struggle to live. From without came the hostility of powerful enemies. On the south and west the Empire was protected by the Sahara and the Atlantic, but on the north and east there were no such natural barriers. There the frontiers had to be held by troops and fortifications. Along the border, German tribes were ever pressing. Julius Caesar in his day had inflicted a shattering defeat on the Helvetii. This brought two centuries of peace. Once again the German tribes, in battle units as terrible as any the ancient world had known, moved towards the Roman borders. They could no longer be effectively repulsed, so the Emperors compromised by allowing selected groups to cross unhindered into Roman territory and settle there as colonists. Many became soldiers in the Roman army. Thus the German barbarians became acquainted with Roman culture. Chief among these barbarians were the Franks along the lower Rhine, the Alemanni further south, the Goths on the Danube and the Vandals near the Baltic. About the year 400 all these peoples were pressing more and more heavily on the imperial frontiers and the weight of pressure increased when the Huns, a savage race of Mongols from central Asia, began to push the Goths out of their new homelands and into Roman territory along the lower Danube. Such was the situation at the end of the fourth and the beginning of the fifth century.

The crisis was not long delayed. On the last day of December in the year 406 a horde of Germanic tribes pierced the Rhine frontier at Mainz, and swept like a tidal wave through Trier, Rheims, Tournai, Arras, Amiens westwards towards the North Sea and the Atlantic. Paris fell and Orléans and Tours. The victorious army passed through Aquitaine to the Pyrenees and then turned eastwards towards Toulouse and Marseilles, devastating as it went. Gaul was left, in the words of a contemporary writer, "one gigantic funeral pyre". By the autumn of 409 the Vandals, the Alans and the Suevi were in Spain. A year later the city of Rome was captured and sacked by Alaric and his Goths. Here was catastrophe in an almost inconceivable form. The world was stunned. We would look in vain for a modern parallel. In a nightmare of impossible horror the imagination might picture the capture of New York by a swift-moving airborne army from the Communist East, but the place of New York in the free world of today is not the place of Rome in the world that was the Roman Empire. When the news of the fall of Rome reached St. Jerome in his cell at Bethlehem, his cry was a note of anguish which comes piercing through the centuries. "My voice fails me," he says, "and the sentences I dictate are broken by sighs and tears. That city which conquered the world has now herself been conquered." In another place he speaks pessimistically of the fall of Rome as the beginning of the end. That judgment was correct: the days of the Empire were indeed numbered.

How could such a disaster have happened? The pagans, still a self-assured and vocal minority, explained it in their own way: the old gods who had given Rome greatness were angry. The people who had deserted them to become Christians deserved no better fate. To prove these critics wrong St. Augustine wrote one of the most famous of his works, *De Civitate Dei*, "The City of God", a remarkable book in its own right and doubly valuable as the first effort of a great mind to appraise the wealth of God's mercy and tenderness of God's love in the management of the wayward human soul.

The story of Europe in the fifth century is the story of the Völkerwanderung, the roving of the innumerable bands of turbulent barbarians. No part of the west was left unmolested. German tribes, generally known as the Angles and Saxons, landed in Britain, occupied within the course of a hundred years most of the country and created what we know as England. Gaul was overrun by the Burgundians, the Franks and the Visigoths. For more than two generations a façade of Roman control was maintained; there were emperors with nominal authority and Roman generals like Aëtius and Aegidius and barbarian Kings like Ricimer and Gundobad, who were content to be regarded as imperial ministers. With the deposition of the last pathetic Roman Emperor, Romulus Augustulus, in 476, the Roman Empire in the West may be said to have ended. It was to continue in an area more circumscribed, in the East, until the fall of Constantinople to the Turks in 1453. But the influence of this eastern Greek-speaking Empire on the West was felt little outside of Italy, and even in Italy was felt but in part and at long intervals of time. As far as western Europe was concerned the Roman Empire was dead. When Chlodovech, King of the Franks, defeated Syagrius the Roman Patricius, at Soissons in 486, the last remnant of Roman territory in Gaul was lost. Henceforth in the West secular history is the record of the fortunes of the barbarian settlers already mentioned, or of new tribes, like the Langobards, who had profited by the general confusion to win for themselves a more comfortable place in the sun.

By the end of the sixth century the situation in western and southern Europe was virtually stabilized. The most remarkable phenomenon in the area was the growth of Frankish power. Already the Alemanni, the Thuringians and the Burgundians had been reduced. Aquitaine and Provence had been captured from the Visigoths and all these lands added to the Frankish kingdom. The Visigoths retained possession of Spain and a small region of southern France round Toulouse. In Italy the long struggle between Justinian and the Ostrogoths had ended in favour of the Emperor, but his victory had merely opened the way for a new invasion of the peninsula by the Langobards. In Africa and the Mediterranean the Eastern Empire had made headway against the Vandals. For southern and eastern Italy and for Rome the Exarch at Ravenna, representative of the Emperor at Constantinople, was a person of importance, but this did not alter the fact that about three-quarters of Italy remained in possession of the Lombards and could not be wrested from their grasp. From the political and military point of view the incident of the invasions was closed; the barbarians had won. The substance of power was everywhere in their hands. A momentous change had taken place.

It was in every respect a change for the worse. Life in the Roman Empire had its drawbacks, but in comparison with the barbarian states that took over from it life in the Empire might be taken as a foretaste of Paradise. The first great benefit lost was peace. Warfare among the German tribes was incessant, and it was warfare attended by unspeakable cruelties. All tribes fought the Romans. When these in time were eliminated, the tribes fought among themselves, the Franks against the Burgundians, the Visigoths against the Suevi and the Vandals, and so on with many varieties of permutation and combination. But far worse were the more local struggles, the internecine strife between king and nobles, between prince and prince, between brother and brother. For the history of the Franks in the sixth century we have the immortal work of Gregory of Tours. It is a history that literally reeks with blood. Even now, after the lapse of nearly fourteen centuries, the pages of Gregory cannot be read without feelings of nausea and revulsion. If I give some details I do so with reluctance, and only because the savagery of the age can otherwise not be understood.

Let us pause for a moment and look at the Frankish dynasty. Chlodovech, or as the French call him, Clovis, was the first king to be converted to Christianity. That was in the year 496. Three years before, he had married Clotilde, niece of the King of Burgundy. He had murdered her father and his own brother, Chilperic. Chlodovech died in Paris in 511, but before his death, he murdered or had murdered all who might prove dangerous to his throne. The ruling prince at Cologne was murdered by his own son; and he in turn had his skull cleft in two while he was entertaining Chlodovech's envoys. By systematically slaying all the princes and relatives of his house Chlodovech extended his kingdom over the whole of France. He was utterly heartless, wily, insidious, capable of a humorous sally at the moment when he was cutting off an opponent's head; and these qualities reappear in his descendants.

Clotilde, the widowed queen of Chlodovech, even when living in semi-religious retirement at Tours, incited her sons to avenge the death of her father and mother. In the course of the war which followed her son Chlodomer was killed, but not before he had caused the ruler of Burgundy to be slain, with his wife and children, and their bodies flung into a well. Chlodomer left three young sons. Clotilde, the queen-mother, took these under her protection. There was thus the possibility that one at least of the three might one day come to the throne. The thought was gall and wormwood to the uncles. One day when the boys, then ten and seven years old, chanced to be in Paris, the loving uncles, Lothar and Childebert, seized them and stabbed them brutally to death. The youngest child, Chlodovald, was saved almost by a miracle. He became a priest, lived the life of a saint and when he died about 560 was canonized. His name, softened into Saint-Cloud, survives in the well-known placename beside Paris. The murderers of his brothers divided the inheritance between them.

Soon enough they were fighting among themselves. Chramn, the son of Lothar, joined his uncle Childebert against his father. Fortune finally turned against the son, who was burnt to death in a hut by his father's orders. When Childebert died, Lothar was left sole ruler of the Franks. His inheritance passed in equal parts to his four sons. These were the contemporaries of St. Gregory of Tours and the story of their dissensions fills many of his pages. Three of them were interested in concubines rather than in queens. The fourth brother, Sigibert, ashamed of these *mésalliances*, sought and obtained the hand of Biunhilde, a Spanish princess, daughter of the King of the Visigoths. They were married at Metz in 566. For the next fifty years Brunhilde was to hold the centre of the stage in the drama of the Austrasian Franks.

And a tragic drama it was. Sigibert had married a royal princess. The prestige which this won for his court filled his brother Chilperic with envy. There was but one remedy: Chilperic in his turn should find a queen of royal blood. His gaze fell on Galswintha, the equal in every way of Brunhilde, for she was her elder sister. There were obstacles to be overcome. Chilperic was by now a much married man. He had repudiated one queen, the mother of three of his children, and replaced her by a serving maid, an able woman named Fredegunda. Her dismissal was a matter of course. Nevertheless the new queen left her home in Toledo with anxious forebodings. Indeed she could hardly be got to part from her mother at all. Again and again she returned to embrace her. Galswintha pleased King Chilperic, not least because of her huge dowry. But the pleasure waned. Fredegunda, the maid, soon recovered lost ground. The queen objected. One morning she was found dead in her bed. This was to be the fate of many others who stood in Fredegunda's way. Brunhilde was infuriated by the murder of her sister. Between her and Fredegunda there could now be no reconciliation. Their quarrel was interminable and in the literal sense, deadly. Human life had no value and

2

the moral law no meaning when they stood in the way of vengeance. Any crime was tolerated if it paid. In 573 war broke out between the brothers and lasted incessantly for forty years. Sigibert summoned help from the fierce pagan Germans beyond the Rhine. Fredegunda had Sigibert murdered by hired assassins. He left as heir a boy of five. When Fredegunda's sons died, in 580, she had a stepson and his mother, a former queen, who for long had lived innocently and harmlessly in a convent, both murdered. Fredegunda sent an assassin to slay Brunhilde and, when this man failed ignominiously in his task, had his hands and feet cut off. She had the Bishop of Rouen stabbed to death while he was saying Mass in his cathedral. When a nobleman courageously rebuked her for the murder and sacrilege she had him poisoned.

In 593 a period of internecine war began, so savage that the worst experiences of the past seemed in comparison to be but insignificant afflictions. The year is important, for by that time St. Columban had settled in Burgundy. King Childebert died in 595, poisoned, rumour said, by his queen. His age at death was 26. Theudebert and Theuderic, his infant sons, succeeded to the kingdom. In 597 Fredegunda died, strangely enough, in her bed. Brunhilde supported her younger against her elder grandson, and to keep her power over the former, sought to prevent his lawful marriage, a crime which St. Columban duly castigated. In a new war between the half-brothers in 612 Theuderic won the victory. Theudebert was taken prisoner and slain. The brains of his infant son were dashed out against a stone.

Theuderic died suddenly at Metz in 613, like his father at the age of 26. Brunhilde at the end was deserted. She sought to escape but was captured, tried for many murders, tied to an unbroken horse by her hair, one leg and one arm, and so dragged over rough ground until she died. St. Columban was still alive, but he was by then an exile in Italy. So much has been said about the Frankish kings and queens to show how badly needed was the work of the Irish missionaries in the Frankish dominions.

With royalty giving such dreadful example it would be too much to expect high moral standards among the ruled. Lawlessness was so flagrant that the question may be asked whether the notion of justice was understood in the Merovingian kingdoms at all. Horrible brawls broke out in church, before the very altar. There is almost no end to the individual acts of barbarism related by Gregory of Tours. Let one example suffice. The abbot Lupentius had incurred the enmity of the Count of Javols. As a result, the abbot was summoned to appear before Queen Brunhilde. He was acquitted but on his way home was attacked by the Count and deprived of his head, which was placed in a bag full of stones and thrown into a river. Not only did the Count go unpunished: soon afterwards he was named bishop of Rodez, where his actions were in keeping with his earlier career. His elevation to an episcopal see illustrates an important truth: when prelates were inflicted on churches by kings and queens not for virtue or learning but as a reward for secular service rendered to rulers the influence of the clergy on the people could not be expected to be far-reaching. In fact it made little impression. Very different was the effect produced by the monks. To them the faithful turned for good example, guidance, disinterested help in the performance of their religious duties. The reality of life was brutal enough; those unable to pay their taxes were cast into prison, where they were kept bound with their feet in stocks. Imprisonment was a universal form of punishment. There were jails and lock-ups in every town and township of France. Debtors languished within them till they paid. Horrible torture was an everyday occurrence; sentence of death passed almost as a matter of whim. In a world so harsh, so unrelenting, so sensual, so inhuman, so brutish, the monastery was the one oasis, where in silence, manual and intellectual work and prayer, the incomparable Christian ideal of faith, compassion, hope, love was kept clear and luminous before the eyes of men.

I have spoken of Merovingian Gaul rather than of other areas because the history of St. Gregory of Tours gives us an unexpected insight into Frankish life. There is no need to stress the fact that compared with the world of the late Roman Empire the world of the Franks was a falling world. And the Franks were generally regarded as the best of the Teutonic tribes. Beyond the Rhine and the Alps, in pagan Germany, Switzerland and Lombardy, the level of civilization was considerably lower. Nor were standards higher among the Anglo-Saxons in England or the primitive Pictish peoples of the Scottish highlands.

The following lectures show how help was brought to the millions of souls in these regions by devoted Irish missionaries. That help was in the form of two gifts of supreme value. One was high moral seriousness, the acceptance of God's law and of the gospel counsels and the putting of these into effect without gloss or compromise. The other was emphasis on the cultivation of the mind. Scholarship is only one degree less necessary to the Church than sanctity. In periods of bloom the two flourish side by side in happy harmony. Looking at the world falling wretchedly around him into barbarism and chaos Pope St. Gregory the Great experienced moods of sadness and even of pessimism. Was the end of all things really at hand? Was the hour coming when no man might work? His fears were justified. But the hand of God is never shortened. A little light was already visible through the darkness, for St. Colmcille was active in Scotland and St. Columban had arrived in Gaul and St. Gall would be soon in Switzerland and the faith which moved them would continue to inspire countless others of our Irish nation to journey abroad and by their labour as preachers and teachers bring peace and salvation to multitudes who otherwise could hope for little on earth and for nothing in the life beyond the grave.

II

SAINT COLMCILLE IN IRELAND AND SCOTLAND

BY REV. TOMÁS Ó FIAICH

SAINT COLMCILLE had the amazing good luck to have records of his life collected and written down by three distinguished ecclesiastics, all of whom flourished within a century of his own time. Unfortunately the one historian among them, the Venerable Bede, was so preoccupied with other parts of Britain that he could spare him only a single chapter. The other two, Cuimine and Adamnan, both Irishmen and both Abbots of Iona when some who had been Colmcille's companions there were still alive, were in a specially favourable position to compile his biography, but, no doubt influenced by contemporary trends in hagiography, they wrote to edify rather than to instruct. However much we may regret these lost opportunities, it still remains true that from the works of these three writers, Colmcille emerges as a clear-cut and well-defined personality, the only Irishman with whom we can really become intimate in an age when his great contemporaries like Finbar and Comgall and Kevin remain little more than names. Later centuries made him the hero of a literary cycle in prose and verse—a vast conglomeration of history, legend, poetry and prophecy —the best parts of which surely bear comparison with the Ossianic cycle for lyrical feeling and vivid expression of the beauties of nature, all given due place in the sixteenth-century compilation undertaken by the Donegal Chieftain, Maghnus O Domhnaill. But while a critical use of these later sources can help to illuminate the man's personality, it is to the early biographers, and especially to Adamnan, that we must go for the main outlines of his life.

Columba or Colmcille was born at Gartan, County Donegal, on the night of December 7th, 521. Through his father, Feidhlimidh, grandson of Conaill Gulban from whom Tír Chonaill took its name, he was in the direct line from Niall of the Nine Hostages, founder of the greatest royal family in Irish history. On his mother's side, he was related to the kings of Leinster. Cousins of his were kings of Ireland in his own lifetime and had he chosen a secular career, it is possible that he might have attained the title of Ardri. There is therefore some point in the delightful story told by Maghnus O Domhnaill of how peace was restored between Colmcille and Ciarán Mac an tSaoir by an angel who reminded Ciarán that whereas he himself had sacrificed nothing for God but his father's overalls, Colmcille had sacrificed the kingdom of Ireland.

Under the watchful guidance of the local priest

Cronaghan, Colmcille took his first steps in sanctity and learning and then entered St. Finnian's monastery at Moville on Strangford Lough where he was ordained deacon. From Moville he passed under the care of another Finnian, the Abbot of Clonard, whose monastic school in the midlands was the training ground for the saints of sixth-century Ireland. It was probably here that Colmcille was ordained priest. Subsequently he became a member of the community of the newly founded monastery of his former school-companion Mobhí at Glasnevin and remained there until the spread of the Yellow Plague to Ireland in 544 dispersed the school.

The Saint's return to the north gave him the opportunity to found his first monastery. A few miles from the prehistoric hill-fortress of Aileach which served as the royal residence of the ruling branches of the northern Uí Néill for several centuries he was endowed with a grant of land by his royal relatives and here arose Colmcille's first and best loved church:

> The reason I love Derry is
>   For its peace, for its purity
> And for its crowds of white angels
> From one end to the other.

After Derry came Durrow whose foundation ought to be placed about the year 553. Other churches followed but it is not easy nowadays to distinguish those founded by the Saint in person from those founded by his disciples and linked together later as a federation of Columban churches under the headship of his successors. Swords, Tory Island, Drumcliff, Glencolmcille have all claimed him as their founder. Indeed the Old Irish Life goes so far as to state that "A hundred churches which the wave frequents is the number of churches he has on the margin of the sea". Because of the fact that Colmcille never took episcopal orders, his monasteries were in the anomalous position of having jurisdiction exercised by an abbot in priest's orders while a neighbouring bishop was called in or one of the monks was raised to the episcopal rank for the administration of those sacraments proper to the episcopal office.

Colmcille's departure for Scotland in 563 has been ascribed in Irish legend to the part played by him in the events leading up to the battle of Cúl Dreimhne. The Saint's refusal to surrender the copy of the Psalter which he had made without its owner's permission, the appeal to Diarmuid, the High King and his over-simplified judgment, the rallying of Cineal Conaill to the aid of their distinguished son, Colmcille's subsequent repentance and the penance enjoined by his confessor Molaisse are all the stuff of drama and poetry rather than matter for the critical historian. Whatever may have been the Saint's connection with the Battle of Cúl Dréimhne, his earliest biographers all make it clear that personal sanctification and the spread of Christ's Kingdom on earth were the motives behind his exile. Adamnan states simply that "he sailed away wishing to be an exile for Christ"; Bede that "he departed in order to preach"; and the Old Irish Life elaborates on these phrases in words which obviously bear the stamp of truth: "When Colmcille had made the circuit of all Ireland, when he had founded churches and religious houses . . . the resolution which he had made from the beginning of his life came into his mind, namely to go on pilgrimage. He then meditated going across the sea to preach the word of God to the men of Alba and to the Britons and the Saxons. He therefore took his departure". His exile was of course later made the subject of some of the most moving poetry in all Irish literature:

> "There is a grey eye
> That looks back upon Erin;
> It shall not see during life
> The men of Erin nor their wives.
> My vision o'er the brine I stretch
> From the ample oaken boards,
> Large is the tear of my soft grey eye
> When I look back upon Erin".

The Island of I, later known as Iona through a misreading of Adamnan's Latin adjective Ioua, became henceforth his home. It is a craggy, wind-swept, treeless island with a single fertile plain on the sheltered eastern side. Here the monks erected their cells of wood and wattles and their simple conventual buildings—the refectory with its fireplace and urn for holding water, the guest chamber, and the church built of oak. From Adamnan we can piece together the daily round of prayer, mortification, study and manual labour which they followed. The Mass was the centre of their worship and the Paschal solemnity then as now the centre of their liturgical year. Penitential exercises consisted mainly of fasting and every Wednesday and Friday throughout the year, except in the period between Easter and Whit, was observed as a fast-day when no food was taken till the afternoon. During Lent the fast was prolonged every day except Sunday till evening when a light meal was allowed. The principal subject of study was the Sacred Scriptures, much of which was committed to memory, especially the Psalms. Adamnan's acquaintance both with the well-known lives of some of the earlier saints and with classical Latin authors suggests that the range of learning cultivated in Iona from the beginning embraced both ecclesiastical and secular literature. Writing was one of the principal occupations of the monks and the community had no more accomplished scribe than the abbot himself. The most important manual work was the annual round of agricultural labours, but metalwork and fishing are also mentioned by Adamnan as usual occupations. The monastic life was a *Militia Christi*: those who adopted it were soldiers of Christ and their arms were obedience, poverty, celibacy, reserve in speech, humility and hospitality.

In stressing the monastic ideal pursued by Colmcille at Iona, we must not overlook the fact that his greatest achievement in Scotland was as a missionary rather than an abbot. Iona was conveniently situated near the borders of two kingdoms—the Christian kingdom of Dal Riada, colonized and ruled by men of Irish race to the south-west, and the still Pagan kingdom of the Picts to the north-east. Into the ecclesiastical organization of the one and the evangelization of the other, Colmcille now threw that burning energy and impetuous nature which had felt circumscribed in Ireland.

His Pictish neighbours were his first concern and Colmcille decided to follow the example of Patrick in Ireland and go direct to their king. Accordingly in 465, accompanied by only a few companions, he began that long journey by land and water up the wonderful valley, Gleann Mór na hAlban, with its long narrow lakes Loch Linne and Loch I and Loch Ness, all now joined by the Caledonian Canal. On arrival at the king's fortress near Inverness they found the gates barred against them. But Colmcille succeeded in obtaining an interview with the king and, despite the opposition of the druids at the court, converted him to Christianity. King Brude confirmed the Saint in occupation of his island home and from that time till his death cooperated in the work of evangelization going on in the highlands and islands. Because of the nature of the territory to be traversed much of the work must have been really an Apostolate of the Sea, and with Cormac the boldest and most skilled of Iona's sailors as pilot, Colmcille and his monks planted the Cross around the Scottish coast and among the Hebrides, the Orkneys and the Shetlands. Adamnan has preserved the names of some of the Scottish islands visited by the Saint and despite their Latin dress it is possible to identify one with the island of Tiree, about 20 miles north west of Iona, another with Eileann Naomh, one of the Garveloch Isles, and a third with Skye, where placenames like Loch Colmcille and Eilean Colmcille have preserved the memory of the Saint's visits until our own day.

But Colmcille did not confine his attention to the non-Christian portion of his new homeland. With Conall lord of the Scottish Dal Riada he was on terms of intimacy. When the latter died in 574 his successor and cousin Aidan assumed the title of King and came to Iona to be solemnly inaugurated by Colmcille. It is the first recorded example in European history of the inauguration of a civil ruler by an ecclesiastical one and it is noteworthy that the rite consisted of an imposition of hands together with a blessing. The kingship of Dal Riada, later to be transformed with the annexation of the Pictish territory by Kenneth Mac Alpin into the kingship of Scotland had begun under Christian auspices, and Colmcille had been recognized by the Gaelic-speaking portion of Scotland as its ecclesiastical head.

The assumption of the royal title by King Aidan made it necessary that the relationship between the Kingdom of Dal Riada and the High Kingship should be clarified. Hence in the following year both Colmcille and King Aidan crossed to Ireland to attend the Convention of Drumceat. Historical writers have been all too prone to suggest that the convention issued what was tantamount to a declaration of independence in favour of the new Scottish kingdom. But as Mac Neill has so astutely pointed out the problem concerned in the main not the Scottish part of Dal Riada but the Irish part, which found itself attached to two independent jurisdictions. Being part of Ireland it was subject to the sovereignty of the High King. Being part of Dal Riada it was subject to the immediate rule of a king over whom the High King had no authority. A conflict of rights and claims was inevitable. As the High King of the day was Aedh Mac Ainmire of the Cineal Conaill, a cousin therefore of Colmcille's, the Saint ought to have been the ideal mediator. But owing to his close friendship with the King of Dal Riada, the High King did not welcome his intervention, and it was left to the High King's brother Domhnall to welcome back on behalf of Cineal Conaill their most illustrious exile. A compromise solution proposed by a young lawyer Colmán was finally accepted which provided that Dal Riada was to serve Ireland with its land forces and Scotland with its sea forces.

Colmcille's presence at the Convention of Drumceat was destined also to have an important influence on the cultural life of Ireland. One of the most burning questions to be decided was the standing of the poetic class in Ireland. Because of their haughty demands and the widespread use which they made of the deadly weapon of satire even against the High King himself, a considerable body of opinion in Ireland favoured the suppression of this secular body of learned men. The emergence, since the introduction of Christianity, of a new body of *literati*, the products of the monastic schools, provided a rival group who were naturally jealous of the patronage afforded to the standard-bearers of a purely secular culture, in its origins not even Christian. The position of secular learning and its schools must have been therefore a critical one. Had not Colmcille thrown the weight of his prestige in their defence they must have surely met an overwhelming defeat from which they would probably never have recovered. As it was, the old order was saved from extinction but stringent regulations were laid down to curb undue demands for the future. Placed henceforward in a favoured position which was clearly delimited in law, secular learning could continue its course parallel to the new ecclesiastical learning of the monastic schools, each assisting and complementing the other but never again rivals prepared to exterminate each other. If the Irish learned classes with their schools of poetry, law and medicine were never again threatened with extinction from the sixth till the sixteenth century, and during that millenium enjoyed a patronage unequalled elsewhere in Western Europe, then to Colmcille "let the greater praise belong".

His return for the Assembly of Drumceat was not the Saint's only visit to Ireland. When the later legend, which looked upon his exile in Scotland as a penance imposed on him by his confessor, had taken root in Irish tradition it became necessary to reconcile his presence at Drumceat with his vow never to set foot again on the soil of Ireland nor to behold her men and women nor to consume her food and drink. Hence the origin of the far-fetched story told with such satisfaction by Maghnus O Domhnaill:—"Bhí fód d'úir na hAlban fana chosaibh an fad do bhí sé in Éirinn—There was a sod of the soil of Scotland under his feet the while he was in Ireland and there was a black cloth over his eyes and his cap was over them in likewise and the cape of his cowl was over them outside . . . And he brought with him from Scotland sufficient of food and of drink so that he would not consume the food or drink of Ireland as long as he abode there". But this late accretion takes no account of another visit of the Saint to Ireland in or about the year 585, when, as Adamnan tells us, he visited his own foundation at Durrow and the neighbouring monastery of St. Ciarán at Clonmacnoise.

Thus active to the end of a long and crowded life Colmcille prepared for death with a series of tender partings which are movingly recalled in Adamnan's splendid final chapter. We can do no better than quote some excerpts from this narrative where the writer throws off to some extent the shackles of his hagiographical models and in simple yet moving terms recalls the saint's preparations for death. He is quoting, he tells us, what he has heard from those who were present:

'He and his dutiful attendant Diarmuid go to bless the granary which was nearby. When the Saint had blessed it and two heaps of corn stored up in it, he uttered these words: . . . Greatly do I congratulate the monks of my household that this year, also, if I should perchance have to depart from you, you will have enough for the year without stint . . . In the Sacred Volumes this day is called the Sabbath which is, interpreted, Rest. And this day is truly a Sabbath day for me . . . And while the Saint, weary with age, rested, behold the white horse, his faithful servant, runs up to him, the one that used to carry the milk pails to and fro between the byre and the monastery. Coming up to the Saint he lays his head against his breast, knowing that his master was soon about to leave him. Returning to the monastery, he sat in his cell transcribing the Psalter and coming to that verse of the thirty-third Psalm where it is written "But they that seek the Lord shall not want any good thing" he says: "Here I must stop at the foot of this page; let Baoithin write what follows". When the Bell began to toll at midnight he goes to the church and falls down in prayer at the altar. Diarmuid then lifts up the holy right hand of the Saint that he may bless the choir of monks. And after thus signifying his holy benediction, he immediately breathed forth his spirit'. It was just after midnight on the morning of Sunday, the 9th of June, 597.

Colmcille had passed from the earth but his name and fame remained. If his real achievements were soon encrusted in legends which have gone on growing almost till our own times—some of the so-called prophecies of Colmcille, for example, came into existence only in the nineteenth century—it is a remarkable fact that this legendary material has only served to accentuate, never to contradict, the main lines of his character, as described by his earliest biographers. It has given him, however, a unique position in the hearts of his people under a threefold title—the poet-scholar, the exiled patriot and the missionary saint.

First the poet-scholar. Adamnan refers often to his work as a scribe and the scribe was the scholar *par excellence* in the Irish monastic system. Whether the copy of the Psalter for centuries carried into battle by his O'Donnell kinsmen and now preserved in the Library of the Royal Irish Academy was really written by Colmcille's own hand will probably never be established, but the attribution need not be rejected on palaeographical grounds alone, as must the attribution to his pen of the Book of Durrow. With Colmcille as a poet Adamnan shows no acquaintance. But the Saint's defence of the poets at Drumceat demanded that he be given at least honorary membership of their fraternity and thus later poets never ceased to put their most elegant religious verses and their most poignant songs of exile into his mouth. Three Latin hymns of considerable beauty are attributed to him and the best known of them, the *Altus Prosator*, has been compared with the *Dies Irae* for its vivid description of the terrors of the Day of Judgment.

Of the poems in Irish attributed to him not a single one can have come from his pen in its present form. Yet the sentiments expressed in many of them are so much in keeping with his character that if not later modernizations of verses originally composed by himself, they may well preserve at least some echoes of the Saint's own words. It is ungracious to call them forgeries for at the time of their composition they were no more forgeries than were, say, the words put into the mouths of historical characters in Shakespeare's plays.

Secondly, and closely related to his poetry, Colmcille has been venerated as the prototype of the patriotic Irish exile never ceasing to yearn for his native land:

> "Dá dteagmhadh éag dála damh
> Is ar mhéad grádha Gaedheal.
> If I should meet death, it would be from
> the amount of love I bear for the Irish".

The literature surrounding his exile therefore became, as Kenney puts it, the first Irish body of formal nationalist propaganda. Small wonder that during the last century emigrants from Donegal spent their last night in Ireland on the flagstone at Gartan which a constant local tradition pointed out as the spot of his birth.

Thirdly, Colmcille is the missionary saint above all others who appealed to the Irish mind. Later missionaries may have gone further afield in their labours; it might be even argued that the personal contribution made by some of them to the spread of the Church and the elaboration of a new Christian culture was greater than his; but their posthumous glory has been left to the races whom they evangelized. Colmcille, however, has always been regarded as a saint of the homeland, where by the early Middle Ages he had already been given a place in the Trinity of National patrons. For centuries after his day no break in culture or social organization separated the West of Scotland from Ireland, and it was in Ireland that the federation of churches linked through his patronage persisted longest and that his legends flourished most luxuriantly.

Of the qualities which pinpointed his sainthood in the eyes of his contemporaries Adamnan gives a brief list in the preface to his work. "He was angelic of aspect, clean in speech, holy in deed, of pleasant disposition, great in counsel. He could not pass even a single hour without applying himself either to prayer or reading or writing or to some manual labour. By day and by night he was so occupied in unwearied exercises of fasts and vigils that the

burden of any one of these particular labours
might seem to be beyond human endurance. And
amid all this he was beloved by all, ever showing a
cheerful holy countenance and gladdened in his
inmost heart by the joy of the Holy Spirit." By
reading between the lines in Adamnan and the other
early biographies we can add to this list. Generous,
warm-hearted, imaginative, capable of the tenderest
affection for his friends and of the most passionate
hatred of injustice and oppression, consumed with
devotion to his native land yet filled with zeal for
the propagation of the Gospel elsewhere, fiery by
nature yet tempering his zeal by constant mortification, he was the most characteristic personification of
the Celtic temperament with its virtues and its fail-
ings, all sanctified in the service of God. To the land
of his adoption he gave the Christian message with
such success that he must surely rank above all others
as the Apostle of Scotland. To the land of his birth
he gave a new purpose and direction in her ecclesiastical life, thus opening the way for the missionary
movement, which was to be the supreme glory of the
Irish Church.

III

SAINT AIDAN IN ENGLAND

BY PROFESSOR J. M. WALLACE-HADRILL

How do we know about St. Aidan? We have no
biography of him, as we have of many other of the
missionaries of the Dark Ages; his letters (if there
were any) do not survive; he leaves no poetry behind
him; and contemporaries have virtually nothing to
say of him. If the brethren of Iona saw the signifi-
cance of his life's work, they did not say so. Even St.
Willibrord, the apostle of the Low Countries and a
devotee of the cult of Aidan's master, King Oswald,
did not think to include Aidan in his calendar,
though a later hand did repair the omission. What
we do have, however, is a witness more precious than
any of these. The third of the five books of Bede's
Ecclesiastical History has a good deal about King
Oswald and St. Aidan; so much, indeed, that it could
be claimed that we do have a biography of Aidan.
Certainly Bede gives more information about him
than we get about the hero of many a saint's *Life* of

greater length; and this is why succeeding generations excerpted the chapters about Oswald and Aidan and allowed them to stand on their own as finished biographical studies.

As we go along, I shall have plenty to say about Bede, the sanest and the humblest of historians, master of many crafts besides, always teaching and always learning. I believe he would have applied to himself some words written centuries later by poor Benjamin Robert Haydon: "every man is a student till he dies, and longer too"; but what does need to be made clear at once is, first, the nature of Bede's evidence about Aidan, and secondly, the factors governing Bede's treatment of evidence at the time of writing. Bede was usually careful to say how he obtained materials for his *History* and what kind of evidence he was using. In the case of Aidan, he cites no written source, and it would be a fair guess that there never was one. What he does cite are the recollections of others; and we must remember that he could have had plenty of first-hand reports. Bede was born about 670 and Aidan had died in 651, so that men who had seen and heard Aidan need scarcely have been in their seventies to have been interrogated by Bede when he was collecting materials for his *History*. After all, Bede could get a reliable second-hand account of the personal appearance of the Roman missionary, Paulinus; and that takes one back to 628. If, then, Bede can make us see Paulinus as he stood there in the mission-field with his stooping figure and emaciated face, black-haired and hook-nosed, *venerabilis simul et terribilis aspectu,* how much more can we trust him when he tells us what sort of a man St. Aidan was. Then, too, we must remember what things were like when Bede wrote. The great days of the Celtic mission were over in Northumbria, the Roman Church had established her sway there (though I sometimes think that we over-emphasize the differences between the two), and Bede was unhappy about the future. His lifetime had seen a wonderful flowering in English church art and architecture and learning, and in missionary work on the Continent; yet he had his doubts, and these we are far too apt to overlook. They are clearly and fearlessly stated in his letter of advice to his pupil Ecgbert, recently promoted to the See of York. I doubt if the Lindisfarne Gospels, illuminated almost under his very nose, would have impressed Bede quite in the way they impress us—I mean, as evidence of a thriving church. But that is another story. My point is that Bede looked back to a golden age, to Aidan's age, a simple time when bishops tramped the roads and kings were their friends.

We speak of Anglo-Saxon Northumbria, and so did Bede; but he always remembered—what we can overlook—that Northumbria was really Deira, an Anglian settlement centred upon York, and Bernicia away to the north, another Anglian settlement with its headquarters in the coastal fortress of Bamburgh. These two, though connected in some ways, were distinct and indeed were for a time separated by a no-man's land of what is now County Durham. It was by no means a foregone conclusion that they were to find permanent political union. It was in Deira, the southern kingdom, that Paulinus settled to preach the Gospel. His mission started from York and is unlikely to have penetrated deep into Bernicia. Whether because Paulinus failed and was compelled to flee south or because his own royal sponsor lived at Bamburgh, Aidan avoided York. If Bede is right, he seemed rather anxious to distinguish his own mission from that of his Roman predecessor. That first Roman effort had disintegrated with the political stability of King Edwin's Northumbria, though I believe it would be safer to think of the Deirans as being thereafter lapsed Christians and not pagans, like the Bernicians. It was in these troubled times that Oswald sought refuge among the Christian Picts who lived over his northern borders in what are now the Scottish Lowlands, men conceivably not less civilized than his own Northumbrians. There, he came under the influence of the Irish monks of Iona; indeed, he may even have stayed with them. At all events, when the chance came to return from exile, one of his first acts was to ask for an Irish bishop to convert his people. Bede gives two accounts of this: Oswald may have approached the Pictish magnates or he may have gone direct to Iona—in which case they seem to have sent him a most unsuitable first choice, who was soon withdrawn (it is right to remember that not all missionaries succeeded). Either way, it does not much matter. What matters is that the initiative lay with the king, who had just won a great victory under the Christian banner. Constantine had once done this, and so had Clovis: these early rulers believed that the proof of the pudding was in the eating. Eventually, then, and probably

late in 634, the Irishman Aidan and a company of
monks arrived from Iona in Northumbria. In the
succeeding twenty years they and their successors
were to convert the Bernicians, reconvert the Deirans
and despatch missions to the English south of the
Humber. It was a colossal undertaking. We have
to bear in mind that it was accomplished not at all
in peaceful times but precisely when Northumbria
stood most under constant threat of invasion by the
great pagan king of Mercia, Penda. How was it
done?

In the first place, it was done through Aidan's
unshakable orthodoxy. I mean, that he never once
departed from the characteristic pattern of Celtic
missionary enterprise. He came with his companions
because he was sent; he came at the behest of a
victorious king, upon whom he utterly depended;
he came to continue his life under an ascetic
monastic rule, just as he had known it in Iona,
though now a pilgrim in a foreign land whose
tongue he never fully mastered. So equipped, he
obtained from the king the Island of Lindisfarne
to be his base and his home. Sir Frank Stenton
thinks he chose Lindisfarne for safety. This I rather
doubt, for the island can be reached easily enough
from the mainland at low water. Others have thought
that he wanted it to remind him of Iona, or to
point the contrast between the York of Paulinus and
the way he intended to live. This, too, I doubt.
The fact is, that Lindisfarne lies not above an hour's
sail from the royal residence of Bamburgh; surely
it was proximity to the king that attracted Aidan?
If we think Lindisfarne hard to come at and a bit

isolated, Aidan found it convenient for frequent
missionary journeys and even too near the centre
of things for peace and quiet. When he wanted to
think, he left Lindisfarne to live for quite long
periods alone on the smaller and much more
desolate island of Inner Farne. Bede, himself a
monk, gets the point; he says Aidan liked going
there to pray by himself and to think quietly; and
still, in Bede's day, they showed the spot where he
used to sit alone. Once, from Farne, he watched
Penda sacking Bamburgh two miles away. It is so
hard to get a clear image of the stark simplicity
of the life of a man living under obedience; and
this, after all, was his whole strength. You cannot
really understand Aidan till you have seen Farne
and assimilated the fact that on that precipitous
reef of black rock, guarded by tide-rips as fearful
as any off the coast of Britain, men have lived for
choice.

After a time, Aidan and his original following
were fairly heavily reinforced from Iona. We may
picture these monks, and probably others who were
not monks, setting out from Lindisfarne on explora-
tory trips into Northumbria, and perhaps north as
far as Edinburgh, but always under the protection
of royal authority. And two other things they owed
to the king; first, the gift of lands where they could
set up oratories and establish what we should call
mission-stations. More than once Bede speaks of
the *villae regiae* or royal estates made available to
them; and we know that other magnates followed
suit. It would be wrong, then, to suppose that the
Irish monks deliberately cut themselves adrift from

the well-to-do and the powerful. Secondly, Aidan owed to the king much personal help as interpreter; for if Aidan did not understand English very well, the king had at least taken the trouble to learn some Irish during his exile. One cannot imagine a directer way of showing that the Christian mission had royal approval. We learn that the monks preferred to journey on foot and not to ride if they could help it. This has been interpreted as a demonstration of personal humility; for it was the privilege of aristocrats to ride, and these Irishmen did not wish to be taken as such, even though some of them undoubtedly were. In the next generation, however, St. Cuthbert had no hesitation about riding, and Aidan himself was prepared to do so if necessary. I suspect that the decision to go on foot may not have had much to do with humility. Bede seems to give a different explanation; he says that Aidan walked so that whomever he met, rich or poor, pagan or Christian, he could pause and converse with. Sometimes he would compel them to meditation upon a psalm or some scriptural reading. He was devoid, says Bede, of *segnitia,* the willingness to let things drift. I myself know a parish priest who, so far from using a car, would not even ride a bicycle for fear of passing a parishioner without a chat. So this explanation seems perfectly satisfactory to me: it is the direct contact between the bishop and his flock that marks the Irish missionary. He is not really a humbler bishop than some of his more ornate successors; he is simply a bishop without a diocese, without parishes, without much in the way of traditions, or books or buildings; in a word, a bishop without frills.

But a bishop, nevertheless; and this is the point when we should look more closely at the characteristics of Aidan's rule that most struck Bede. Bede had his own ideas about bishops. In his biography of St. Cuthbert, he gives a picture of one kind of bishop—you might call him the type of the Celtic bishop with an appreciation of *Romanitas*; in his *History* he discusses more briefly a type of bishop who had learnt his trade on the Continent (St. Wilfrid, namely); one of his closest associates was Acca, Bishop of Hexham; and at the close of his life he wrote a long letter to his old pupil, Ecgbert of York, to instruct him in a bishop's duties as he saw them. Now, it was Bede's opinion that the bishops of his own day by no means came up to standard; they were becoming over-concerned about worldly affairs; they were ruling dioceses far larger than they could efficiently manage; they were turning a blind eye to such scandals as the setting-up of bogus monasteries on private property; they were not making enough use of royal support. These are specific charges based on direct observation. We may call Bede an idealist if we wish; but that is how he saw things and he cannot be brushed aside. In part, at least, his ideal was that set forth by his hero, Pope Gregory I, in a little book called the *Liber Regulae Pastoralis*. Here, the great pope had put down quite simply the moral duties of the pastor and had insisted (what seems obvious enough now) that a bishop must first live a good life if he hopes to lead his flock in the same path. But it is not so obvious if you consider the overwhelming doctrinal and disciplinary preoccupations of the Early Church. Looking back to the missionary days of the Northumbrian Church, Bede could not help recognizing the pastoral qualities he learned from Gregory's book in the lives of Aidan and his followers. Being an Irish monk, Aidan had no special regard for the hierarchical position of a bishop; to him an abbot was a greater figure. But he recognized that a bishop must lead the kind of life he preaches; and this is what Bede liked about him. It is the moral qualities of Aidan that speak to Bede: his *mansuetudo*, or gentleness of disposition; his *pietas*, or sense of duty; his *moderatio*, or regularity; above all, his *discretio*, or discerning prudence. These are difficult words and I am not sure that I have conveyed their full import. But at least it is certain that Bede chose them with care. Let me illustrate the moral quality of Aidan with two stories from Bede.

The first is as follows. One Easter Day, King Oswald and his bishop sit down to dine. A silver dish is set before them (no doubt an import from the Roman world; the barbarians loved such things). It is laden with delicacies. Both stretch out their hands in blessing, but at that very moment an official comes in to report that a great many beggars had arrived and were demanding alms. It is the king who at once sends out the silver dish to them; they are to enjoy its contents and then divide the silver between them. There is nothing unusual in this; silver dishes were always being broken up in the Dark Ages. What is noteworthy is Aidan's

reaction. Delighted by this act of *pietas*, he seizes
the king's right hand and exclaims "May this hand
never grow old!" And according to Bede's information, the king's hands, later chopped off when he
fell in battle before Penda, were preserved as relics
in the Church of St. Peter at Bamburgh. The point
of the tale is that Oswald was a very great king, a
warrior of renown over whose tomb the monks of
Bardney were to hoist his war-banner; and yet he
knows, and Aidan knows, what Christian *pietas* is.

The second story concerns King Oswin of Deira,
to whom Aidan attached himself after the death of
Oswald. Oswin had given Aidan a horse to use when
crossing rivers. A poor man meets the bishop and
begs alms, and Aidan, full of pity, gives him the
horse with all its royal trappings. Later, as they were
on their way to dinner, the king, you may think
reasonably, asks the bishop why he had handed over
what was a special and costly personal gift when
there were plenty of lesser horses to give to the poor.
Aidan's reply is quick and characteristic: "Do you,
then, hold the son of a mare dearer than the Son
of God?" But this is not the end of it. They enter
the hall and the bishop takes his place at table;
but the king, who has been hunting, stops to warm
his hands at the hearth with his thegns. Then suddenly, recalling the bishop's words, he ungirds his
sword, hands it to a thegn, and then runs to the
bishop and falls at his feet, asking forgiveness.
"Never again", he says, "will I speak of this or question how much of my money you give to the sons
of God". Aidan, however, is not pleased. He is
alarmed. He forgives the king and begs him to sit

down and forget about it and be happy; which the king does. But the bishop gets progressively sadder. When at last his chaplain asks him, in Irish, what the trouble was, he replies: "I know that the king is not to live long. I have never before seen a humble king, and so I know that he must quickly die; for his people are unworthy of him." Shortly afterwards, the king met a cruel death at the hands of his kinsman, the King of Bernicia. Twelve days later, Aidan himself was dead. "I have never before seen a humble king"; this is the moral quality that astonishes Aidan, even to tears and to prophecy. It astonishes Bede, too.

These two stories, as I have said, illustrate moral qualities. They also illustrate that intimate trust between king and bishop without which no missionary work of this age ever succeeded. One thinks of St. Boniface among the Germans, troubling his head about whether he really ought to mix with the fast-living Frankish set at the court of his protectors, so that the Pope had to say to him, in effect: "My dear fellow, cease being so literal about things. See what side your bread is buttered, and make the best of a bad job." Aidan never made this mistake, and so we find him not only on excellent terms with successive Northumbrian kings but equally with their magnates, who give generously to him for the poor and for the redeeming of captives from slavery (an important matter, this, in the seventh century) though he never spared them or compromised over essentials. It was just the way he had with him, and what I can only call his transparent sanctity, that made this possible. There is never any hint of his being agin' the government, or Irish in a way that the English could not take (St. Boniface was English in a way that nearly drove the Franks crazy). This is why he can attract great ladies, like Heiu of Hartlepool and Hild of Whitby, to take the veil and found nunneries, and why he can gather round him disciples of the quality of Wilfrid, Chad, Cedd and Eata. One can hardly conceive of four men more different in temperament; but he was the master of them all.

One thing Bede could not overlook in Aidan. This was his resolve, son of Iona as he was, to stick to the Irish way of reckoning the date of the movable feast of Easter (the one great feast of the early Christian year). He would not have it that the Romans were right about this and the Irish wrong. This was a question of discipline, not of doctrine; but it mattered very much, since in a court where the queen followed one practice and the king another, there might be a discrepancy of a whole week between the two celebrations of Easter. Ultimately, in 664, matters came to a head in Northumbria, and at a meeting at Whitby, the king ("smiling to himself" says Bede) decided for St. Peter against St. Columba. But all this was kept quiet during the episcopates of two of the three successive Irish bishops of Lindisfarne: namely, Aidan and Finan. They were too well loved. Only during the reign of the third, Colman, did the cloud burst; and Colman withdrew, first to Lindisfarne, and then to Ireland, taking some of the bones of Aidan with him to Iona. Bede does not overlook this stumbling block of Easter, but he is charitable about it and observes that, in celebrating his Easter, Aidan kept in his heart the very things that we keep in ours. How could one be more magnanimous? In the same paragraph, he writes that, though he cannot overlook this shortcoming, he is going, like a true historian (*quasi verax historicus*) to praise whatever was praiseworthy in Aidan's life, to the profit of his readers. It would be ungenerous to suggest that the increased importance of the Pictish Kingdom in Bede's day would have made any slighting of the first Irish mission impolitic.

Aidan died on a royal estate near Bamburgh, where he had a mission-centre. He died in a sort of tent or lean-to, propped against a buttress of the church wall. The date was 651, the last day of August. His body was taken to Lindisfarne for interment in the little monastic cemetery, though, later on, he was re-interred in the new stone church. Had he lived another decade he must have witnessed the clash between his own church and that of Rome. He would not have liked it. But was it defeat? The witness of Bede is quite clear on the matter; the work of the Irish monks in England was a permanent gain; it was more—it was a point of reference in a troubled world. Christianity had at last struck deep roots in the North, and popular veneration was Aidan's reward. Most Roman of Englishmen, Bede looked back upon the career of Aidan and saw there the roots of his own Christianity.

IV

SAINT COLUMBANUS

BY MARGUERITE-MARIE DUBOIS

SAINT COLUMBANUS, the most fearless, perhaps, of all the fearless Irish saints, is no stranger to my listeners. He is, in fact, one of the brightest ornaments of Ireland's apostolic crown and his name must surely be familiar to all his fellow-countrymen.

It will hardly be necessary, therefore, for me to tell you that he was born sometime during the sixth century, the exact date being vague. Nor need I recall his family, of which very little is known, except to say that his destiny was revealed to his mother in a prophetic dream. So from his tenderest years he was marked with the seal of the Holy Spirit. Because of this, at an age when youth blossoms forth into frivolous adolescence, Columbanus felt himself drawn to a higher vocation and decided to abandon the world for the cloister. The decisive words spoken by a holy woman hermit fixed him on this choice. Nothing could shake his resolution from that day forward, even the opposition of his mother who threw herself at his feet entreating him to give up his plan.

Steadfast in his determination and supported in some miraculous way in what he set out to do, Columbanus spent some time in each of the two of the most famous monasteries in the country: Cluain Inis whose prior was Sinell and Bangor which was under the direction of Comghall.

There, in these two havens, among chosen people, was shaped the militant and priestly soul of this great soldier of Christ. Ordained to the priesthood, fully versed in things human as well as divine, humanist and theologian, he learnt to unite and make inseparable two seemingly conflicting sides of spiritual life—contemplation and action. Surely in this dual nature of his vocation must we seek the distinctive mark of his strength and influence.

The young monk spent many years gaining experience of conventual life. A life of prayer first and foremost! In the shadow of the cloister he learnt the consummate art of prayer. He came to possess fully this mystic habit of the soul which, under the influence of grace, unites itself with God more and more each day. He trained himself for this union in the hard school of detachment, abandonment and love. It is not surprising that during these hours of recollection he found the secret of spiritual life—a secret that he bequeathed to his disciples and to us all in a simple formula: "Let him be filled with God who wishes that his prayers may all come true. . . . Blessed is the soul wounded by love, for in its wounding it is always healed." This high ideal of unitive prayer was the early fruit of his sanctity; it was soon to become the keystone of his apostolic life.

More than ever, now, Columbanus heard the missionary call and his pioneering vocation became too strong to resist. Towards the end of the sixth century he left Bangor, bringing with him twelve of his fellow-monks. After an exhausting sea journey the heroic band reached the shores of Brittany. Without wasting any time they proceeded to preach the gospel to the pagan people who crowded round them. Their success was so immediate that word of their learning and piety reached the king of Austrasia, Sigebert. He summoned Columbanus to his court and there the Irishman convinced him that he brought to Gaul not only the inestimable treasures of the faith but also the benefits of culture and civilization. The king was won over by his words and the Irish monk was authorized to set up his headquarters in a suitable part of the king-dom to be selected by himself. Having searched for a time, Columbanus chose the Vosges March-land, a territory which enjoyed a certain measure of political independence. Here in the silence of the woods, close to gushing springs, he laid the founda-tion of his first abbey, Annegray, on the ruined site of a Roman fortress.

On this spot, the French Association of the Friends of Saint Columbanus have conducted excava-tions in recent years. They have brought to light Merovingian foundations and some mediaeval tombs, deeply moving in their primitiveness. So can we see to-day, on this same ground, traces of that

Columban way of life so long extinct. In the light of our own endeavours we can better understand the difficulties which confronted the original builders. And we can appreciate more clearly too, the scenes described by Jonas, who wrote the life of Columbanus. We can visualize the famine of the severe winters; the invasion by wild beasts which the saint learnt to tame; the back-breaking working which produced only a meagre harvest; the long journeys to preach the gospel; the sermons and the conversions—in short everything that made of this human enterprise a centre of divine life.

Soon the community increased in numbers and the reclaimed wasteland became too confined to accommodate a fast-growing monastic family. Columbanus searched for a new location and found first Luxeuil and later Fontaines.

Luxeuil, founded in 590, was to become the most brilliant centre of learning and virtue in the Middle Ages. It is to an Irish saint that France owes this priceless distinction. This vast monastery acted as a centre of gravity between Annegray and Fontaines. It sheltered within its walls a multitude of monks, craftsmen, lay brothers and scholars. The most varied trades were represented there, constituting a wonderful asset to the social life of those hard times. Talented masters taught there and far from confining themselves to the study of religion they liked to cultivate literature and even medicine in the form of a simple pharmacopoeia. In short, profane culture was not despised by Saint Columbanus but went hand in hand with religious teaching.

It is easy to imagine what marvels of will-power

and organizing spirit were implied by the existence of an establishment like this in such a backward and poor country. The burden of responsibility often weighed heavily on the shoulders of the founder. At such times he sought refuge in solitude, hoping to draw new strength from meditation and hear more clearly in the silence the voice of the Lord.

The cave where he used to hide, at the top of a hill beside a spring which had welled up miraculously, can still be seen. Contemplating it, we can imagine the saint's retreat from the turmoil of community life where he could still remain in contact with the monastery. We can follow too the train of his meditations. Perhaps it was in the secret of this isolated spot that he composed his most beautiful prayers—"Inspire us with Thy charity, O Lord, that our loving quest for Thee may occupy our every inmost thought; that thy love may take complete possession of our being, and divine charity so fashion our senses that we may know not how to love anything else but Thee."

It was in this quiet resort that the holy man planned and perhaps even wrote the books of guidance which described in detail the lives to be led by his monks. Columbanus is the only sixth-century Irish saint who has left us a collection of religious writings which enable us now to determine the character of saintliness of the Irish church in early mediaeval times.

The importance of this fact will be readily understood when we realize that the writings of Columbanus constitute a primordial link between the early Church's faith and practice and the structure of its spiritual life. Thanks to these canonical or theological texts, we can reach into the soul of a man who was a product of his time and can discover the essential ideas which were the basis of his spirituality.

The Rule of Saint Columbanus falls into two parts: the first part being a guide to doctrine for the use of monks, while the second is more concerned with the maintenance of monastic discipline. The first part places the accent on the obligations of religious life conceived in accordance with the principles of the Gospel. It treats of obedience, silence, mortification, poverty, humility, chastity, prayer and prudence. This monastic rule for living constituted even then the "path of counsel" as suggested for the elect rather than being the "path of precept" intended for all Christians. But because his book was aimed at chosen souls, whose destiny was perfection, Saint Columbanus did not content himself with formulating counsels but also laid down precepts. He did not ask, he insisted; he commanded rather than recommended, imposed obedience to the law rather than docile acceptance of grace. He exacted love of God rather than rested content with preaching and exhortation.

The second part of his rule governs the exterior conduct of monks and their relations with others. It underlines the observances of conventual life in detail and prescribes frequent confession for minor defects as well as for more serious faults.

This fundamental aspect of Columbanus's theology extended beyond the monastery walls and concerned lay folk in the world outside. Wise and virtuous priests were chosen as confessors or as "anamcharaid" (soul friends) to whom the faithful could turn. In this way the chief emphasis was shifted from public to private penance and absolution. The greatest importance is attached to the renewing, healing and fortifying powers of confession. The spiritual director becomes a guide and a doctor of souls just as much as a judge; and the frequent use of the sacrament of reconciliation emerges as an essential way toward spiritual development. It is to Saint Columbanus that we owe this important contribution to the theology of penance, as we know it to-day, in the theory and practice of the Universal Church.

Nevertheless, the Columban penitential appears to modern commentators as unduly severe in its sanctions. Perhaps one should distinguish two aspects in this matter. The first concerns monks, that is those whose business is perfection. Why should one wonder that such people should be required to show unceasing heroism and unfailing adherence to the law? Why be shocked if the slightest departure from this law is punished as a mark of treason towards God, as a breach of promise towards a supreme Master, as an inexcusable transgression of the renunciation and submission solemnly accepted and professed. The other aspect concerns Christians in general. Here the punishment is in proportion to the crime. For example, a murderer does penance for ten years, a false witness or perjurer seven years, an adulterer three years, a thief one year. Now, if we compare these penalties with those imposed by the modern penal code, they will seem slight. Let me remind you that in France we punish murder with death or life imprisonment, false oath and false witness with five years imprisonment and theft with one to five years. The basic difference is that the civil code imposes a restraining penalty without amending the criminal whereas the penances suggested by Saint Columbanus were accepted voluntarily and accomplished piously before pardon came to reinstate the reconciled penitent in the Christian community.

Saint Columbanus's success in shaping souls is also due to the practice of frequent communion—an innovation in his time. He gave as a precedent for this custom the practice of the early Christians, who received communion every time they attended Mass and he made of this Divine food the indispensable nourishment for those who wish to live a fervent Christian life.

Thus the call to purity through confession, to reparation through penitence, to love through communion constitutes the very symbol of Columbanus's teaching as well as a new and vivifying contribution to the spiritual conscience of the Church.

But Saint Columbanus was no mere legislator. He took care not to neglect the social responsibilities imposed upon him by his role as abbot and evangelist. So he railed against the leaders of this world, solicitous to crush their evil inclinations and to bring them back to the path of virtue.

Queen Brunehaut and King Thierry lived loose and scandalous lives. Columbanus invoked all his authority to rebuke them for their excesses. But he was totally unversed in the art of diplomacy. Unrelenting, severe, intimidating, he was more accustomed to exhorting, reprimanding and threatening than he was to mollifying and ingratiating. Although he emerged victorious from many controversies, it eventually came about that a cleverly constructed plot drew down upon him the anger of Gaulish sovereign and clergy. Thereupon new fuel was added to the old quarrels provoked against the Irishman by the court and the local clergy. There were plenty of arguments against him. For one thing, Columbanus tenaciously upheld the traditions of his country; Irish tonsure, observance of the earlier non-Alexandrine cycle in determining the date of Easter; adherence to strict enclosure within the monastery precincts. The plot against him thickened and the courtiers who had so often felt the lash of his tongue incited the prince against him. Then one day the break came.

King Thierry demanded harshly that the monastery should be open to all. In a fit of rage he himself violated the cloister. This was more than the patience of Saint Columbanus could stand. With a frightening glance he looked the king up and down and then gave expression to one of those terrible prophecies which alas were certain to be fulfilled.

"If you have come to destroy our monasteries and violate our rule, be it known unto you, your majesty, that your kingdom will be destroyed and your race destroyed with it."

In making such an audacious threat, Columbanus was signing his own extradition warrant. Only the exile's road was open to him now and in spite of interventions from Providence which enabled him to escape from his guards he still had to resign himself to leaving Luxeuil. Accompanied by his Irish brethren he took the road that the Lord showed him.

After a long journey which sapped their strength, although it was punctuated by many miracles, they reached Switzerland. At Tuggen, a town lapped by the waters of a lake, they decided to pause for a while. As soon as they had set up their camp they began to reconnoitre the surrounding country. Their first attempts at evangelizing proved satisfactory but excessive zeal soon spoiled their success. Faced with the hostility of the natives who had designs on the missionaries' lives, they had to resign themselves to flight. Sick at heart, Columbanus sought new territory where he could plant the cross of Christ. His choice fell upon Bregenz; but new trials awaited them there.

"This land," the abbot used to say, "is a golden cup filled with serpents." Before long political events made life precarious for the monks. They could not safeguard their establishment, so once again prudence dictated a hasty departure.

Columbanus was now visited by an angel who pointed out to him the next goal he must try to reach. Thus taught he turned his steps towards Italy. It was a painful task indeed for these ageing men to climb the Septimer Col, a height of over 7,500 feet. It is hard for us to imagine their endurance and heroism.

At long last, harassed and weary, the little band reached Milan, the end of a long stage in their journey. Agilulf, King of Lombardy, welcomed them with great warmth and allowed them to settle in one of the most favourable locations in the Appennine mountains. So it was that the year 614 saw the founding of Bobbio.

From Bobbio, the last but not the least of these foundations, the extraordinary influence of the Irish monk radiated over the whole of Italy. Here, too, the saint taught his highest lessons.

Rendered gentle by age, strengthened by the unfailing gifts of the Holy Spirit, Columbanus now appears to us in the full light of his sanctity. Deeply marked as he was by the doctrine of St. Augustine, devoted to the traditionalist teaching of Eusebius and nourished on the Scriptures and the books of the Fathers, he conducts himself as a theologian without making any claim to the title. In fact, his doctrine ranges over the whole field of Catholic truth. He discourses on the dogma of the Holy Trinity and the Divinity of Christ; the supremacy of the Apostolic See of Rome; the virginal motherhood of Mary; the power of the keys; the real presence in the Eucharist and the indefectible unity and visibility of the Church. Even in the heat of his keenest controversies with the Papacy, he never lost his sound sense of orthodoxy. His was the theology which Patrick brought to Ireland from Rome. Columbanus now restored it intact and free from all taint of schism or heresy to the bosom of the European communities. He is never blinded by his ardour in defending a point of view which to his eyes seems unassailable. He remains lucid and submissive to the Eternal Truth, never ceasing to be the respectful son of the Common Father.

What can one say further of his profound nature, of his manly heart? His rough exterior hid great generosity, keen sensibility, profound goodness. Columbanus lavished on his friends and brethren unselfish and generous affection; he knew how to share suffering and joy, how to encourage and support. In short, he knew how to love.

It was at Bobbio, however, that the physical decline of his active frame began. Old age came and with it ill-health. God had decided to call home His servant. After a short agony, Columbanus the Great entered into eternity at dawn on the 23rd of November 615.

If the activity of this monk had been purely human that fateful date would have marked for us the end of his story. But Columbanus was no mere man; he was above all the spokesman of God and from his ashes life sprang forth anew.

It was the dawn of a Golden Age for the Church, Bobbio flourished and prospered. To-day alas it lies deserted. From the first century of its existence it became an intellectual centre of surpassing importance. The learning and holiness of its monks were the glory of Northern Italy; the wealth of its library astounded humanists all over the world. To-day we can get an idea of its original splendour from its most famous manuscripts, which are preserved in the Ambrosian and Vatican libraries. An attempt is now being made by Italian scholars to restore this library. It is a consoling thought that the impact of Saint Columbanus has given rise not only to such past glory but to such laudable activity in our own time.

The names of Saint Columbanus's disciples are so famous that we cannot properly pass them by without some reference. Here we must content ourselves with mentioning a few of the most famous. Saint Eustasius and Saint Walbert were directors at Luxeuil of the divine office—that uninterrupted canticle of praise which Columbanus had inspired and prescribed. Desle, abbot of Lure, had come from Ireland with the first group of brethren. Gall founded the famous Swiss abbey of St. Gall which was the cradle of mediaeval learning in Germany and Switzerland. Urcisin built Saint-Ursanne and Sigisbert built Disentis. Valéry, gardener of Christ, was patron-saint of the artisan town of Saint-Valéry. Amé and Romaric were founders of Habend. Faro founded Sante-Croix, Philibert was abbot of Jumièges and Wandrille of Fontenelle. Fara, abbess of Faremoutiers, owed her vocation to the call of Saint Columbanus. Of three brothers, blessed by the hand of Saint Columbanus, Ado was abbot of Jouarre, Ouen was founder of Rebais, and Radon was a benefactor of Reuil. Add to these many celebrated bishops and saints, renowned in different fields: for instance, Amand of Maestricht, Arnould of Metz, Aubert of Cambrai, Chagnon of Laon, Didier of Vienne, Donatus of Besançon, Eligius of Noyon, Ermenfroy of Verdun, Léger of Autun and myriads of others.

It was the dawn of a golden age for the Church, an age of faith, of culture and of heroic virtue. Historians have recorded the names of sixty-three immediate disciples of Saint Columbanus whose influence spread all over Europe. If we trace this expansion on a map, we shall see how it embraces the north and east of Gaul as far as the Rhine; Belgium, Germany, Bavaria and Switzerland and down as far as Northern Italy. Everywhere the land is dotted with monasteries. The monks clear away the undergrowth, build new houses, elevate and transform souls, re-construct the world. How widely is all this known or how fully realized? Have our contemporaries any idea how much modern science and morality are indebted to these pioneers of the Middle Ages and above all to this Irish saint whose name is too seldom heard?

For it was not the will of God that the Columban rule should last as such for ever. For four centuries the disciples of Saint Columbanus ruled men's lives in the monasteries of Europe. It raised the Christian ideal to sublime heights of asceticism and renunciation. But it failed to outlive the rude age for which it was designed. Yet, even when the gentle Rule of Saint Benedict replaced the Irish rule, the early Columban foundations still retained the integrity of strict observance. It was thanks to this original discipline which was so severe and so often criticized that these monasteries were able to dispense with the reforms which were a recurring feature of mediaeval monasticism.

In our day, with the return to favour of the cult of Saint Columbanus in France, Italy, Switzerland and America, a new era is opening up under the aegis of the great Evangelist. A chapel has been erected in his honour in the crypt of St. Peter's in Rome and his statue occupies a place of honour in the National Shrine of the Immaculate Conception in Washington. At Lourdes, the Secours Catholique has placed one of its houses under his patronage. His missionaries from Ireland carry his name to the most distant parts of the East. In recent times we even have had a French Minister of Foreign Affairs, Robert Schuman, referring to Saint Columbanus as "the patron saint of those who seek to construct a united Europe." Furthermore, at a time when the re-union of the Churches seems to be so ardently desired, Saint Columbanus might well be chosen as the zealous apostle of the Ecumenical Movement. In his letter to Pope Boniface, he deplored the schisms which then were disrupting Christian unity; he ardently wished for understanding and harmony in peace and charity; he longed to gather together in the same fold, under the same crozier, the reconciled flocks of the one and only Shepherd. For, as he vigorously recalled, "we are members of one body, the Body of Christ, and we should rejoice together in the unity of Faith and in the knowledge of the Son of God."[1]

Let us make it our wish that his Holiness Pope John XXIII, who in 1950 celebrated at Luxeuil the virtues of its first great abbot, may place under this saint's protection the apostolic work of the Ecumenical Council. No one more than Saint Columbanus deplored the lacerations of the seamless Cloak, the symbol of Unity; nobody is more fitted than he to repair the rents in that sacred garment or to reunite in the one Faith and the one Church the children of the one Divine love.

[1] Ephes. IV. 12-13.

V

SAINT GALL IN SWITZERLAND

BY LUDWIG HERTLING, S.J.

At the point where the Rhine leaves the Alps it forms a lake, one of the largest and most picturesque of the European continent: the Lake of Constance, which the Germans call Bodensee. To-day three countries meet at this lake: Germany, Austria, and Switzerland.

From its southern shore a two hours' walk brings you to the town of Sant Gallen, St. Gall's Town, centre of the Swiss Kanton St. Gallen as well as of the diocese of the same name.

St. Gall is considered the patron not only of this part of Switzerland, but of the whole of the neighbourhood of the Lake of Constance. You find his name attached to places like Sant. Gallenkirch on the Austrian side; and in the two German dioceses of Freiburg and Rottenburg, north of the Lake, there are over forty parish churches dedicated to this ancient Irish saint.

Who then was St. Gall?

St. Gall belongs to the group of Irish monks who started from Bangor, under the leadership of the great Columban, and brought into being on the Continent a new religious movement in France, Northern Italy and Southern Germany. It was in the last years of the sixth century, at about the same time that Pope Gregory the Great was sending the first missionaries from Rome to the South East of England. But the Columban movement on the Continent spread more rapidly and much more widely than did Pope Gregory's in England; this at first developed rather slowly and only later was to bring forth abundant fruit.

St. Gall then was one of the first companions of St. Columban. In history his figure is somewhat overshadowed by that of the great apostle, with whom he shared for the best years of his life, joy and sorrow, success and disappointment. It is only in the last years of his life that we have some knowledge of the disciple as a figure distinct from that of the master.

This is not to say that we must put St. Gall among those saints of olden times whose life is wholly legendary or whose very existence may indeed be open to question. No. St. Gall is an historical personality in the full sense of the term. He is mentioned in the *Life of St. Columban* by Jonas of Bobbio, in the seventh century. Furthermore we have two accounts of his life written by Benedictine monks of Reichenau, an abbey on the Lake of Constance. One of these biographers was the famous Walafrid Strabo. It is true that he wrote not much earlier than the year 800, but it is no less true that he based his work on an older biography written in barbaric Latin of which fragments are extant. So, if the sources are not ideal, they certainly are no worse than those of many other historic personalities in those remote centuries. In a word, we may be certain of the main events in St. Gall's life.

The first thing we know about him is that he was brought by his parents to the monastery of Bangor in Co. Down. In those days and for many centuries afterwards there was the strange custom of offering children to a monastery, to be educated there in the hope that they might become monks themselves later on. It seems strange to us, because we find it unjust to fix a child's career in life, even if that career is a sacred vocation, without his own free consent. But in those times the parental power was almost without limit. The parents thought themselves entitled to decide for their children whom they should marry, or whether they should enter the Church or whatsoever else might be calculated to bring the children benefit, and everybody, the children included, found this right and natural. It must be remembered that in those days to send a boy into a monastery to become a monk did not mean anything like ill-treatment or imprisonment; rather it was a way to put a boy on the highest rung of the social ladder.

From the fact that Gall was presented by his parents to the monastery of Bangor we can infer two important facts; first that he was born in Ulster, because parents as a rule did not send their children far away but brought them to a monastery in their own neighbourhood. Secondly, we can conclude the approximate time of his birth, otherwise nowhere stated. Bangor was founded by St. Comgall in 558/9. So Gall could not have been born before 550, even if he were offered to the monastery as a child in the first year of its existence. On the other hand when Gall accompanied St. Columban to the Continent, about 585, he was already a priest, which means that his age then was at least thirty. So he cannot have been born earlier than 550 nor later than 555.

Of all the years Gall spent in Bangor we know nothing save that his master and instructor was Columban, a monk, considerably his elder. Columban was not the abbot of Bangor but rather what in later times would be called master of novices. Gall seems to have made good progress in studies and religious virtue under so austere a master, for later he was considered a good Latin scholar and was chosen for the priesthood, a distinction then rather rare among the monks.

About 585 occurred the great event which was to give quite a new direction to Gall's life; the departure of Columban from Bangor and his journey to the Continent.

It was not unusual for a group of monks to set forth from their monastery to make a new foundation. The popularity of monastic life in these days in Ireland was such that famous houses like Bangor soon became overcrowded and some of the monks had to find a home elsewhere. But in this case the stimulus to move was different; it was the missionary ideal, the desire of men like Columban not only to make new foundations but to do good to souls and where necessary to convert the infidel. Columban and those who shared his inspiration wanted to promote the kingdom of God by planting monasteries where they were needed and where hitherto there had been none.

All Columban's travels have this double aspect; in the first place he was looking for some lonely spot in which to build a monastery, because in those days a monastery was regularly in the wilderness, an outward symbol of its break with the world. On the other hand they had to be within reach of neglected Christians or outright pagans so that the monks could exercise their zeal by doing spiritual good.

Of the twelve companions whom Columban took with him when he set out from Bangor, the only one who is more than a name to us is Gall. He seems to have been Columban's right-hand man. The little group tried to do missionary work first in Brittany and Northern France. Finally they came to Burgundy and settled down in an ancient Roman fortress called Luxovium, or in French Luxeuil. That was about 590. Luxeuil was destined to become a great monastic centre. From the beginning many Burgundians came to take the monastic habit. Soon there were two daughter convents, Annegray and Fontaines. Everything seemed to be going well.

Then fell the cruel blow. Columban was banished from Burgundy by the king or rather by his mother, the powerful Brunhilde. We do not know exactly the reason why. Almost certainly it was because of his strictures on the king's immoral life. Anyhow he had to leave the country and with him the Irish who had come with him from Bangor (and were still alive). All the monks of Luxeuil wanted to accompany him into exile. This was forbidden by the Burgundian government which wanted to pre- serve Luxeuil as a monastic centre; they could control it without difficulty, they thought, when the Irish were gone. It was about the year 610 that Columban, already in old age, and Gall, now over fifty, had to set out again in search of a new home. Columban would have liked to go to Italy, but the Burgundian government insisted that he should travel towards the west. They sailed down the Loire (by ship). In Tours they paid their tribute of devo- tion at the tomb of St. Martin. They reached Nantes on the Atlantic at last, from where they could easily have sailed back to Ireland. This, in fact, they never did. With the help of Chlotarius (II) of Neustria, as the western part of France then was called, they turned their faces again towards the east. They journeyed through Paris and the Rhine- land and finally were directed by the King of Austrasia to move up the Rhine into what is to-day Switzerland. They had completed an immense circle and were not so very far from Luxeuil; but they were beyond the reach of the Burgundian govern- ment.

In those parts the old Rhaeto-Roman population, for the most part Christian, had become very scarce. The lands were just then being occupied by the Alemans, a German tribe, not very numerous as yet, and largely pagan. There was plenty of no- man's-land, especially in the mountains. Thus it was easy to find a site for a monastery, and there was plenty of missionary work to be done. The short time spent by St. Columban and St. Gall together in Switzerland is almost the only part of their lives that we know of in some detail. It would appear that they were then alone. Looking for a suitable place in which to build a monastery, they went first to the Lake of Zurich, and thence to the Lake of Constance where they found a local priest called Willimar. He received them kindly and assisted them in their further efforts.

Once Columban and Gall happened upon some heathens who had gathered around a large barrel containing beer. It was a genuine barrel with hoops and held, as the old life of St. Gall records, 26 bushels. They asked what it was for and were informed that it was to be used for a sacrifice to the God Wodan. Columban blew on the barrel which responded at once by bursting and spilling on the ground all the precious beer. The heathens seem to have been more astonished than angry. They said to Columban: "Goodness! What a breath that was!" This event induced some to become Christians. Another story told by Walafrid is this. Gall burnt a sort of wooden temple and threw the sacrificial gifts which it contained into the lake. This time the heathens were fiercely angry. They assaulted St. Columban and tried to kill St. Gall.

All in all, it seems that the methods of the two missionaries were drastic rather than effective. After a year or two of hardship and disappointment, St. Columban decided to leave the Lake of Constance

and go to Italy, which had always been his wish
ever since he had been driven from Luxeuil.

There may have been another reason. The Burgundian king, Theoderich, Columban's old enemy,
had by this time conquered his brother, Theodebert,
King of Austrasia, and in consequence had become
ruler of all Gaul and Burgundy, including the
Alemanni. The result was that Columban, even if he
had nothing to fear for his personal safety, could see
no possibility of settling down in Switzerland in
territory that was held by the king who had driven
him out of Luxeuil.

Columban therefore decided to set out for Italy,
but just at this moment Gall fell sick with an
obstinate fever. To travel while it lasted was out of
the question. St. Columban was not quite convinced
of this. He rather suspected that St. Gall was lacking
in fortitude, was chary, perhaps of new adventures.

Perhaps Columban was not quite astray in his
judgment. St. Gall, at any rate, learned to like the
country. He had acquired some mastery of the
language of the Alemanni, and may have hesitated
to leave them so abruptly. This is not to suggest
that his sickness was feigned; he was really and
truly ill, with a high temperature.

Columban at first was disposed to use his authority.
Only when Gall knelt and implored him not to do
so, did he give in and allow Gall to stay. At the
moment of parting came a stern abbatial joke "Cum
hilaritate animae." "I have a good mind," St. Columban said, "to forbid you to say Mass from to-day
till the day I die." To impose even such a severe
penance would not be out of keeping with St.

Columban's character, but the two were Irishmen and friends and the twinkle in the abbot's eye would have negatived the menace in his words.

So Columban moved to Italy and St. Gall remained at Brigantia on the Lake of Constance, sick and sad and disconsolate after the departure of his beloved master. The year was just after 610.

Gall soon left Brigantia and crossed the lake, back to Willimar the local priest of Arbon. Under the care of this good friend he regained his health and began to look for a new place where he might commence his monastic life.

Help came from Willimar's deacon or curate, Hiltepolt by name, a great fisherman and hunter, and therefore well acquainted with the paths across the mountains. Hiltepolt guided the stranger in his search for a suitable place for the cell or monastery. He showed Gall a beautiful empty valley between high mountains, with plenty of fresh streams containing trout. This last was important, for at that time the monks never allowed themselves meat and were therefore dependent for part of their food supplies on fish. Gall liked the spot. He planted there a wooden cross adorned with relics of saints as the sign of his taking possession. Here he intended to build his hermitage or cell.

At this point we are struck by the discrepancy or at least what looks like a discrepancy, between missionary zeal and love of solitude. Why, we may ask, if Gall wanted to stay and preach to heathen Alemanni, did he shut himself in an isolated valley? Or again, if he wanted to serve God in solitude and prayer, why did he not follow his master to Italy as soon as he had regained his health? Or why did he not go back to Luxeuil?

The answer, of course, is that missionary work, or even parish work for that matter, was not then as it is to-day. A missionary did not need to live in the midst of his flock. There were no catechism classes to be held, no confraternities and sodalities to be directed, no Catholic action. A missionary could live all the time in his cloister, with his religious community, dividing his time between prayer and work. There would be in the convent priests who preached in the church to the people who came and otherwise provided for the spiritual needs of the local population. In other words, there was a minimum of what to-day we would call parish work and pastoral care. This looks to us rather a primitive method of evangelization. But we must not forget that in those days it was a successful method. Most parts of Europe were brought to the Christian Faith in that way. What induced the heathens to become Christians and the bad Christians to become good Christians was, perhaps, not so much the sermons these monks preached as the example of their lives entirely devoted to God.

Such a man was St. Gall, from the moment he had occupied his cell at the source of the river Steinach, exactly where the city of St. Gall now stands. Gall was a monk, abbot of a growing community and, as such, a figure whose fame for holiness was spreading through the mountains and through the whole district, round the Lake of Constance.

When the daughter of the Duke of the Alemanni fell sick, her father called in Gall to pray over her

SAINT GALL IN SWITZERLAND 69

and give her his blessing. Gall came, and the girl became well at once. The Duke's gratitude knew no bounds. He loaded the holy man with gifts and wanted to make him bishop of Constance for the see had just then become vacant. Gall refused. But in order not to disappoint the good Duke he promised to write to Columban in Italy and ask for instructions.

That he could write such a letter to Columban is not as odd as it sounds. There was no post, of course, in those days. But there were always travellers, clerics, monks, merchants, who could carry a letter from Switzerland to Burgundy, from Burgundy to Italy. The monasteries were permanently in communication with one another. Gall knew that Columban had arrived in Italy and had there founded among the part pagan, part Arian Longobards the monastery of Bobbio near Piacenza. We do not know what Gall wrote to him. Probably he told him that he was now head himself of a flourishing monastery and that the Alemanni wanted him as bishop. There would be no intrinsic difficulty, for many Irish monks were possessed of the higher order, but St. Gall would not be likely to accept were he not assured beforehand of St. Columban's approval.

The answer was not the one he expected. Columban was no longer among the living. He had died at Bobbio on the 23rd November, 615.

We can imagine St. Gall's feelings at the news of his old master's death. He had now no pretext for refusing the mitre, though refusal was evidently his wish. And the Duke of the Alemanni was quite in earnest about it. He called a synod, a meeting of all the prominent ecclesiastics and laymen under his rule. They were anxious to raise St. Gall to the See of Constance. But Gall, who could not avoid being present, found a new reason for not accepting; he was a foreigner, he said, and custom, if not law, demanded that bishoprics be given to a native of the country if one fully qualified were available. He proposed one of his monks, John by name, then a deacon and a native of Raetia Curiensis, that is to say Eastern Switzerland. So John was made bishop of Constance and Gall went home to his monastery, glad to be spared the heavy duties inseparable from the episcopal office.

All this must have taken place in the year 616, the year following St. Columban's death, when St. Gall was about sixty years of age.

There is only one thing more we know of the last years of his life; the monks of Luxeuil sent him a request to return to Burgundy and be their abbot.

After St. Columban and St. Gall had departed at the sword's point from Luxeuil in 610 the remaining monks had chosen as abbot Eustasius, a Burgundian. The king had no grudge against him. Under Eustasius Luxeuil continued to grow and to expand. Its community sent members as missionaries to the Alemanni and to the Bavarians and these apostles on their way eastwards passed by St. Gall's monastery. Thus it is easy to explain how they knew all about his settlement. He was, of course, known to many in Luxeuil as Columban's companion and in that sense as a co-founder of the mother-abbey. In the meantime Burgundian politics had undergone a change. The old queen Brunhilde, who had grown hostile to the Irish, was dead. Thus when the Abbot Eustasius died in 629 there was no reason why Gall should not return and take over the rule of the parent house. This enjoyed pre-eminence if not some form of control over all the monasteries that followed the rule of St. Columban. The number of these was already great.

For Gall it would have been a glorious reinstatement. Nevertheless he refused. There was an obvious reason; he was over seventy and may have had a presentiment of his approaching death.

We would like to have details of his last hours, but they are not forthcoming. All we know is that he did not die in his monastery for the end came while he was on a visit to his old friend, the priest Willimar, at Arbon, on the southern shore of Lake Constance. His body was brought back to the monastic church and there it lies, an object of veneration through all the centuries (since) down to our own day. From this holy Irish monk the picturesque Swiss town and the surrounding canton take their name, St. Gall.

Walafrid Strabo says St. Gall was over ninety years old at death. It is, however, probable that he died about 630, when his age was 70 to 75.

Such is the meagre history of the Irish saint whose memory to-day is treasured by the people round the Lake of Constance, who revere him as their apostle, the man to whom they owe their faith in Christ, their country's heavenly patron. Of his character, his personality, his virtues, his special devotions we know next to nothing. For he left no writings, no window through which we could get a glimpse into his soul. He certainly was very different in temperament from his great master and spiritual father, Columban. St. Columban was a pioneer, a prophet, a legislator, a born leader of men. He welcomed conflict even with bishops and with kings. St. Gall on the other hand seems to have been mild and meek in spirit, unassuming, unambitious. He was no less intent on the service of the Lord than was his master Columban, but service for him would take a different, if equally heroic form.

St. Columban was a man of action; St. Gall was a man of contemplation, a monk by nature as well as by grace. If St. Columban may be compared with St. John Baptist, St. Paul and St. Bernard, St. Gall may be compared with St. Benedict and St. Francis de Sales. You all know that in Suabian hands and under the rule of St. Benedict, the monastery of St. Gall was to rank for centuries among the great monastic centres of the world.

VI

VIRGIL OF SALZBURG

BY PAUL GROSJEAN, S.J., BOLLANDISTE

THERE is no need to exert oneself to find something interesting to say about Virgil of Salzburg. He was an exceptional man, well above the rank and file of Irish monks and missionaries on the continent of Europe in Merovingian times, when Christianity there was at a very low ebb, before the reform of faith and morals associated with the name of Charlemagne. He was indeed less a reformer than a scholar, an administrator and a preacher to the heathen. With a few exceptions, however (one of these being Saint Columban, 150 years before Virgil's time), the ordinary missionaries were forgotten, or survived only as bare names. Virgil was remembered.

He is one of the very small band of Irishmen who obtained the supreme honour of formal canonization by the Pope, though this was to happen some five centuries after his death, because miracles were taking place at his tomb. On June 10th, 1233,

Gregory IX, the Pope who had befriended Saint Francis of Assisi, canonized Virgil. The Roman curia was not very clear about his history; about, for instance, his Irish origin and his title, for he is called Archbishop of Salzburg, though the see had no metropolitan rights in his day.

His real name was Fergal. Being a scholar, he would write Fergil—with an *i*—like several among his contemporaries, to make more close the resemblance with the name of the Latin poet. In Latin it became Virgilius or Vergilius. He was a monk and a priest, already deeply grounded in scholarship which included mathematics, when he left Ireland for the love of Christ. He went into exile, as so many did in his time, with an idea, perhaps, of devoting himself to spreading the faith among the pagan nations of far-off Germany.

In 742, or at latest shortly after 743, we catch a first glimpse of him at Quierzy on the Oise, in Northern France, at the court of Pippin the Short, then mayor (or chief minister) of the palace to the last Merovingian king, Childeric III. Pippin, in the next few years, was to dethrone the Merovingian, and to found the Carolingian dynasty. Charlemagne, Pippin's son, was still an infant in arms.

The friendliness between Pippin and Virgil may be an invention of later writers. It is a fact that Virgil was then sent to Bavaria (a distant part of the kingdom, where Pippin had been waging war for some time), in company with Odilo, its duke. Was Virgil supposed, by his presence and good advice, to prevent further trouble between the duke and the mayor of the palace? Or rather, as was shrewdly remarked, was Virgil selected by Odilo, preferably to some Anglo-Saxon priest or bishop of Pippin's entourage, just because he was neither Frank nor Anglo-Saxon—and therefore less likely to prove a political agent of Pippin, as Saint Boniface and his helpers openly were? Bishop John of Salzburg died in 745, thus leaving Virgil, who was abbot of the monastery of Saint Peter's, the most prominent churchman in the country. Possibly Pippin, who was fond of manipulating episcopal elections, sent Virgil to Bavaria as bishop-designate. But his choice hardly pleased Saint Boniface, who would have preferred one of his friends and disciples, and certainly a prelate of more pliable nature.

Little did Virgil care for the obstinate obstruction offered by Saint Boniface to his appointment, an obstruction that deprived him of episcopal consecration until June 15, 755, when the great organizer had already been a year in his grave. Virgil took his stand on Irish customs. He was content to wield the power in Bavaria as abbot, while remaining a priest. A neighbouring Irish prelate, Dub Dá Crích, who was at the same time abbot of Chiemsee, was only too glad to confer, in Virgil's stead, the sacraments reserved to bishops, Confirmation and Ordination.

Such arrangements, it appears, were not a novelty in Bavaria. The predecessor of Bishop John, whom Virgil succeeded, Saint Rupert, had been both bishop of Salzburg and abbot of Saint Peter's in the same town. Thus he had followed Celtic customs rather than the strict regulations which Boniface later enforced.

The tension between Saint Boniface and Saint

Virgil was serious. It led, not merely to the refusal of consecration, but to a series of incidents which show in Virgil a man of too deep learning and too wide views to be quite understood by his contemporaries, his superiors included. Virgil did little or nothing to relieve the strain.

First, there was a dispute about the form of words used in baptism. Boniface requested Pope Vitalian to dismiss Virgil, on the ground of heresy, because the abbot of Salzburg did not object to a priest, somewhere in the inaccessible Alpine valleys, baptizing in *nomine Patria et Filia et Spiritus Sancti*. Two words in the formula are, of course, execrable Latin (*Patria* for *Patris,* and *Filia* for *Filii*), far below the standard of Nursling, where Boniface had been educated and where he had taught "in the best schools". But in spite of the high-brow objection to ungrammatical language, combined with genuine British contempt for native shortcomings, Boniface did not have his way. The Pope and his advisers themselves resorted to strange Latin forms in their daily intercourse with the common people in Rome, possibly even in their sermons. They concluded that the whole matter was one of pronunciation: the good priest in the Alps spoke Latin in the way of his country. This, by the way, is the earliest known specimen of a language still heard in parts of Switzerland, Austria and northern Italy, a depraved sort of Latin melting into the language of the peoples who, in a few centuries, would talk Italian or French or Provençal. It is known to philologists as Rhaetic, Ladin, Romansh, Friulian,

according to the dialect. The Pope refused to con-
demn Virgil on this count. Sad to relate, a recent
writer misunderstood the story and ascribed this
piece of bad Latin to Virgil himself, who was
certainly a better speaker and writer of Latin than
most Merovingian bishops.

But Virgil could use debased Latin on occasion
to serve a purpose. He did this once in order to
side-track St. Boniface. It followed another dispute,
pertaining to science this time rather than to theology, about the Antipodes—the people on the other
side of the earth. Virgil believed in their existence
and said so openly—perhaps, indeed, provocatively.
Now, in Boniface's imagination, the earth was flat
as a pancake. It was unthinkable that anybody
should go round the rim, so to speak, and reach
the nether side, a journey anyway that would have
to be undertaken head downwards. Therefore no
men lived on that side: such people could not
belong to the human race, could not have been
created by God and saved by Christ. Virgil was
heretical on this count also. In fact, with the best
minds of his time, including Bede (who had died
some fifteen years before, but whose writings were
but partly known to Boniface), Virgil followed the
ancients who visualized the earth as a sphere or
globe. Nor was Virgil foolish enough to suppose,
on the other side of the earth, another sun and
moon, as he was reported to do. In any case, he
failed or disdained to make himself understood and
the matter took a serious turn. It must be said
that at this time some queer heresies were burgeon-
ing in the Frankish kingdoms. One of the men

denounced to Rome was a prophet who claimed frequent, almost daily revelations. Another carried about a letter allegedly written by God or by Christ Our Lord, and sent down from Heaven on an altar in Jerusalem. Others supported sundry immoral practices.

Virgil, however, succeeded in countering Boniface in this matter also. The way he did it is perhaps not quite in keeping with modern notions of publishing. He resorted, it would appear, to a literary stratagem, the use of a nom-de-plume. Dr. Heinrich Lowe, a German scholar, was the first, in 1951, to suggest that this is what Virgil had done.

The pen-name was Ethicus Ister (which I understand to mean "the Philosopher from the Danube", though Dr. Lowe takes Ethicus to be "a man from Ethica Terra", Tír Heth, in Irish, that is to say, Tiree, in modern Scotland, not so far from Iona). Under that name he put forth a treatise on Cosmography, a description of the Universe, derived, it was contended, from a Latin version made from the Greek text by Saint Jerome, 350 years before. The tract contained much information about the earth and its wonders (including, of course, the Antipodes), vouched for by the irrefragable authority of the most learned among the Fathers of the Church.

How could anyone *prove* that the authority invoked was a mere figment? There existed at the time no bibliography, no list of authentic works by Saint Jerome. What of the style? If anybody thought of making the necessary comparison he would find himself checkmated. Ethicus Ister had taken the

precaution of pretending that the original trans-
lation had been much corrupted by some Merovingian copyist. He wrote a tolerable imitation of such
things as "Fredegar's Chronicle" and mis-spelt Latin
in unheard of combinations. As a final effort at
concealment he threw in a whole paragraph of abuse
of Ireland, Irish schools, Irish books and Irish
masters.

The publication of the Cosmography apparently
put out of court all objections to the doctrine of
the Antipodes. Yet more, it enjoyed fair success as
a work of reference for recondite geographical information during the next four or five centuries.

Very little is known with certainty of Virgil's
episcopal activities. He was present at the Synod
of Dingolfing, about the year 770, and was thus a
party to establishing a league of prayer or confra-
ternity between Bavarian bishops and abbots.

On September 24, 774, he proceeded, at Salzburg,
to the transfer of the remains of Saint Rupert to
their place in the newly built cathedral, which was
then solemnly consecrated. He deserves praise for
the evangelization of Carinthia, conquered by Duke
Tassilo in 774. Though prevented, possibly by old
age, from taking an active part himself, as he would
have wished to do, he sent thither the monks of
Saint Peter's at Salzburg and these worked under
his control and orders and with his encouragement,
with the monks of Kremsmünster and of Innichen.
The two monasteries just mentioned were founded,
probably through Virgil's influence, by Duke Tassilo
in 769 and in 777.

In the evening of his days, according to the writer

of his *Vita,* the Irish bishop of Salzburg undertook
a visitation and circuit of his vast mountain diocese.
As he came back to his cathedral city, he was over-
powered by the beauty of the country, and exclaimed
with the Psalmist: "This is my resting place forever,
here I will dwell." I well believe it. That verse was
a familiar one to the early Irish pilgrims and missionaries. But I am afraid the Bavarian writer misread
the circumstances: generally, that verse is put in
the mouth of a saint, not on the eve of his death,
but when for the first time he espies from afar the
spot chosen for him by God Himself, round which
angels hover.

Virgil died in the year 784, on November 27,
which is kept as his feast day. He was buried in
his cathedral. His body was found again in 1181,
when work was in progress for a new building. I
mentioned already his canonization in 1233. The
relics were placed in an elevated position on an altar
apart half a century later; and once again still more
magnificently in 1315. When a third cathedral was
erected on the same spot, in 1628, the holy relics,
with those of Saint Rupert, found a resting place
under the magnificent baroque high altar.

Fresh information about Saint Virgil of Salzburg
has been accruing during the last few years, with
the result that certain minds felt it difficult to admit
that the same man was responsible for everything
that was, or was thought to be, his work. Thus, a
German-American scholar, in 1927, found it more
convenient to postulate the existence of no less
than three Virgils, all of them Irish and all living
in Bavaria or its neighbourhood in the eighth cen-

tury. First and foremost came the saintly bishop of Salzburg; the other two were heretics and wanderers. Whatever did not come up to the approved standard of piety and devotion was the work of either of these.

It must be admitted that Virgil was quite a different type from the normal missionary bishop in the time of Saint Boniface. He was a man difficult to order about, a survival, so to speak, of a period when personal values, originality, individuality found full scope in the no-man's-land of barbarian Europe. The time of settling down had now come for the Church in these lands. Boniface was an organizer, with most of the characteristics that were later to make the great British administrator in foreign lands. He insisted on getting his way. Virgil was not always convinced that this was the best and, within the limits afforded by higher authority, took steps accordingly.

While the entourage of Boniface was eminently respectable, one might almost say, *Victorian,* Virgil and his friends were characterized by a many-shaped variety of pursuits and a general unpredictability of conduct. Those of us who studied Old Irish remember that some of the most ancient sentences are glosses of a dreary kind, brief explanations of difficult words or sentences in standard school books like the Latin grammar, the Psalms, the Epistles of Saint Paul. In spite of their linguistic interest and philological importance, they hold nothing out of the ordinary. They form part of a methodical teaching for beginners. There existed, however, as an advanced department of Scripture and Theology, a whole Irish and Celtic tradition very different in tone from the glosses. It survives in Latin, the language of the learned. In spite of the heavy loss of manuscripts which followed on the abandonment of that kind of lore and the predominance, in the Carolingian period, of another school of theology, a long list has been compiled of works, most of them still awaiting an editor. One of those that made its way into print gives in its very title an idea of these studies: *De Mirabilibus Sacrae Scripturae*, "On the Wonders of Holy Writ". Quite recently, the *De Mirabilibus* has been shown, not only to be Irish, but to be a specimen work from a scholarly circle, rather famous in the seventh century, around the monastery of Lismore in County Waterford.

A similar centre of study seems to be slowly emerging at Salzburg, of all places, or in its neighbourhood. Only last month I was told of a forthcoming edition of the *Liber De Numeris*, "The Book of Numbers" (found in Scripture). Various arguments, one of them based on the homeland of the first copies, go to show that it possesses all the characteristics of these early Bavarian manuscripts.

I should not wonder if a similar place of origin were discovered on the Continent, for other collections of texts, which are unmistakably Irish. Such, for instance, are the homilies or sermons in a manuscript of the Vatican Library which came eventually from Fleury-sur-Loire, a Benedictine monastery of central France, where a good many writings from Landevennec in Britanny found a home in the tenth century.

However, more tangible associations lead us

directly to the person of Virgil of Salzburg. One of them is the Fraternity Book of Saint Peter's of Salzburg, a list of persons (living and dead) for whom that community undertook to pray. The original volume is still preserved in the archives there, just as it came out of the hands of a German scribe who could have written under the very eyes of Virgil himself.

A curious feature of this list, the implications of which have been set forth only this year, is that it exhibits the complete catalogue of the abbots of Iona, from Saint Colum Cille to the fifteenth abbot, Slébténe, an exact contemporary of Virgil. The name of Saint Patrick stands at the top, the name of Saint Columban (of Luxeuil and Bobbio) and of Saint Cíarán (of Clonmacnois) are thrown in for good measure. Most worthy of attention is the spelling of Irish names, perpetuating the pronunciation, as taken down by a German scribe from Irish lips—a rare feature at such an early period.

Some scholars had supposed that here was a link between our Virgil and Iona. He had been, they thought, a member of the celebrated island monastery in the Hebrides. This, however, is contradicted by a deeper examination of the source. The catalogue of abbots in the Salzburg manuscript is a list manipulated to make it conform to official history, as opposed to what may be called the real history. Nobody will believe that Virgil, if he had been at Iona or in one of the dependent houses in Scotland or in Ireland, could thus have definitely suppressed all evidence of difficulties in which he had himself participated. The same list, with other subsidiary

considerations, shows also that Virgil, before he left
Ireland for the Continent, was not, as had been
supposed, abbot of Achad Bó, the foundation of
Saint Cainnech: the name of the great patron of
the house, Cainnech, is conspicuously absent.

This led on to another discovery about Virgil of
Salzburg, possibly a faint clue to the region of
Ireland where he came from. By an ingenious piece
of reasoning, it was shown last year that a certain
manuscript prayerbook, now in the Public Library
at Orléans and coming from Fleury-sur-Loire, origin-
ated in fact not in central France but in Bavaria,
and that it had been written for Virgil's successor in
office at Salzburg, the German Arn or Arno, a friend
of Alcuin. When teaching in the imperial schools of
Charlemagne, Alcuin had composed, in rather in-
different and stilted Latin verse, a set of inscriptions
for the altars and relics in his friend's cathedral, and
the names of saints occurring there were found to
tally with a long litany in the Fleury prayerbook.

Some of the names had been collected for his
devotions by Arno, a little time before, when he was
abbot of Elnone (now Saint-Omer, on the Scarpe,
in northern France). They formed a distinct section.
There was, on the other hand, a double group of
Irish saints, which most probably had been inherited
by Arno from the litany recited by his Irish predecessor, Virgil.

Most noticeable was a trio of Irish virgins: Brigit,
Ita and Samthann the first two of whom occurred
both in Alcuin's inscriptions and in Arno's litany,
while Samthann was mentioned in the litany only.
No one would wonder at the names of Saint Brigit

(† about 525) and of Saint Ita († about 575), since these, from time immemorial, had been the most popular of Irish female saints.

But Samthann, abbess of Cluain Brónaig, was quite another matter. She had died on December 19, 739, barely three years before we catch our first glimpse of Virgil on the Continent, at the court of Pippin the Short. This, undoubtedly, was a personal devotion of Virgil to a saint whom he might have known.

There is very little information about Virgil's genealogy or the part of Ireland from which he came. If, by any chance, he had been a relation of Saint Samthann, he might possibly have been entrusted to her as a small boy for his first education. Such childhood memories could be the reason for his remembering Samthann in his prayers, far off in the valley of the Salzbach.

Of such a recent saint, there would not yet be any relics in Salzburg. This would explain why she had no altar consecrated to her name in the cathedral and why there is no mention of her in Alcuin's metrical inscriptions. Besides, Saint Samthann was an all-Ireland figure, well known and influential through the width and breadth of the land, from Tallaght, beside Dublin, to Corco Duibne, the Dingle peninsula in Kerry.

The occurrence of Saint Patrick in the Book of the Fraternity of Salzburg, at the head of the Irish saints, might tell us something too: Virgil would have come from a church or a district where Saint Patrick was specially honoured as the first and chief of Irish saints.

VII

SAINT CATHALDUS OF TARANTO

BY FATHER CANICE MOONEY, O.F.M.

In June 1960 I had the privilege of visiting a city that claims an Irishman as it patron saint, yet is rarely visited by an Irish tourist or pilgrim. It is Taranto in the south of Italy, whose patron is the elusive Cathaldus, with whom this talk is concerned.

The city was founded about 708 B.C. and became the capital of Magna Graecia, that part of southern Italy colonized by the Greeks. It was conquered by the Romans in 272 B.C., destroyed by the Saracens in A.D. 927, captured by the Normans in 1063. At times it was a great mercantile city, at times a great cultural centre. It wilted and prospered under many masters—the Greeks, the Romans, the Ostrogoths, the Byzantines, the Normans, the Swabians, the Angevins, the Bourbons. It is now an important town and seaport of about 150,000 people.

The so-called Old City, the part of chief interest for us, lies on an island, connected with the modern city by a revolving iron bridge, and, with its small piazzas, quaint porticoes, and dark alleyways, is comparatively unchanged from mediaeval times. In the Old City is the Cathedral of St. Cathaldus, which dates back in the main to the second half of the eleventh century. His relics and a silver statue of him, to which we shall refer again, are kept in the large elaborately decorated chapel on the epistle side, which is called *Il Cappellone di S. Cataldo*.

My Irish nationality secured for me a warm welcome everywhere in Taranto. *"Ma lei é concittadino di nostro S. Cataldo"*, "But you are a fellow-citizen of our own St. Cathaldus", I was reminded on several occasions. When I asked the way in a city bus, a group of Tarentines ended up in an altercation in their anxiety to be of help. One man, not a native of Taranto, told me of a popular hymn in honour of St. Cathaldus in his part of the country and offered to procure for me the words and music. Others told me of various places where Cathaldus is honoured by dedications or pilgrimages. When I went to the railway bureau to arrange about travelling back to Rome, Signor Umberto Pupino, the official in charge, on hearing where I came from, decided to call it a day. He closed up his books, handed over charge of the bureau to a colleague, and brought me on a tour of the city. We visited the cathedral together and the sacristan threw open for our inspection the ancient crypt whose pavement Cathaldus himself may have trod.

Signor Pupino suggested I should consult the diocesan archives, but Archbishop Ferdinando Bernardi is eighty-six years of age and bed-ridden and

Auxiliary Bishop Guglielmo Motolese was not available that morning and my time was limited. Yet I was not disappointed because I had already ascertained that they contain nothing that would throw any further light on the historical Cathaldus.

My guide had spoken of *L'Anello di S Cataldo*, The Ring of St. Cathaldus, but had forgotten to show it to me. Deciding that I could not leave Taranto without seeing it, I set out once again from Corso Umberto for the Old City. I had been told I must approach the cathedral and then look out towards the sea. Failing to discover it, I asked a passer-by. At first he thought I was looking for some sort of a gold or silver ring, but he explained that he was a native of Naples who had settled in Taranto only a short time before. We stopped another passer-by. Without an instant's hesitation he made a right turn and exclaimed triumphantly, "Eccolo, Behold it out there a stone's throw from the pier!" Sure enough, it was plain to be seen. A ring of fresh, clear water bubbling up in the sea from a submarine spring. "That's the Ring of St. Cathaldus," he explained, at the same time presenting me with a little coloured picture of Cathaldus which he produced from his pocket-wallet. "On his way back from the Holy Land, the saint took the episcopal ring from his finger and threw it into the ocean there to calm a storm."

I turned a little to the north and there on land I saw a massive statue of Cathaldus, facing towards the sea, his hand raised in blessing. It was erected in 1935 by the present archbishop to petition the heavenly protection of Cathaldus on the port of

Taranto and all who use it. I examined the picture I had been given. It showed a big, blue-eyed, fair-skinned, white-bearded Irishman, with mitre, crozier, and archiepiscopal pall, his hand raised in blessing, and in the background some Roman and Byzantine buildings. I read the prayer in Italian on the back. It began, "Luminous star of Ireland, and wonderful apostle of Magna Graecia, O holy Cathaldus . . ."

"Are there many people here called Cataldo?" I asked a bookseller. "Many?" said he, "why, it's full of them!" I left Taranto with the impression of a man, dead some twelve hundred years, whose memory was as green as if he had died but yesterday. Rarely have I found such an intimate, personal devotion to a saint and patron, with the exception of the Irish speakers of our western seaboard when they speak of Brighid and Columcille and Mac Dara.

But a more remarkable fact about the cult of Cathaldus is how it has spread throughout all Italy, over to Sicily and Malta, and even into the heart of France. He shares this popularity with his fellow-Irishman Columbanus, but I think that the cult of Cathaldus is more widespread in the northern half of the Italian peninsula than that of Columbanus in the southern half. There are or were churches or chapels in honour of Cathaldus at Cremona, Modena, Venice, Bologna, Rimini, Roccaromana in the Campagna, Barletta in Bari, and Lecce, as well as at the following places in Sicily: Nicosia, Palermo, Enna, and Gagliano Castelferrato. Several communes throughout Italy, a number of parishes, and the episcopal sees of Taranto and Cariati look to him as their patron. Altars dedicated to him are to be found in Genoa, Naples, and elsewhere; statues and paintings of him throughout Lombardy, Tuscany, Lazio, the Abruzzi, Puglia, Potenza, and Sicily. An image of him dating back to the latter half of the twelfth century will be found on one of the pillars of the Basilica of the Nativity at Bethlehem.

Near Medina in Malta there is a crypt of St. Cathaldus, adjoining which is a cemetery. At Cottanello in the province of Rieti there is a tradition that he lived at one time in a grotto nearby, which was later converted into a church. At Supino in the province of Frosinone there is a shrine in his honour to which flock numerous pilgrims on March 8 and May 10. At Corato in Puglia a fair held on the week preceding May 10 took its origin from the immunity enjoyed by the town during the great plague of 1483. Legend has it that the saint himself appeared to a worthy citizen of the town and promised immunity if they would promise to erect a church in his honour. At Gagliano Castelferrato during the month of August the people have a custom going back to mediaeval times of offering some of the fruits of the harvest to the saint.

A large-scale map of Italy will reveal an astonishing number of places and geographical features that bear his name. There are, or were, districts called S. Cataldo in Modena, near Viterbo, and in Borgoforte in the province of Mantua, and a few also in Sicily. A stretch of land near Formia is called Contrado S. Cataldo, and an area near Gorgoglione in the province of Matera is called Regione S. Cataldo. Quite a number of farmsteads are marked S. Cataldo or Masseria S. Cataldo. There is one, for example,

near Viterbo, another on the road between Isernia
and Fornelli, another near Poggiorsini. There is a
Taverna S. Cataldo in the province of Naples, a
bridge of St. Cathaldus on the road from Taranto
to S. Giorgio, Bagni di S. Cataldo, literally The
Baths of St. Cathaldus, but now actually part of the
commune of Bella, in the province of Potenza. A
neighbouring wood is also called after Cathaldus.
About eight miles from Lecce in the heel of Italy,
facing the Adriatic, are St. Cathaldus's port, light-
house, and bathing place. Not far from them is a
stretch of reclaimed land called the Bonifica di S.
Cataldo. On the shore of the Gulf of Taranto is a
well of St. Cathaldus which is credited with remarkable curative properties. Legend says that it was
there Cathaldus rested after his shipwreck. There
are two villages in southern Italy known as Case S.
Cataldo, literally, The Houses of St. Cathaldus, and
there is, of course, the well-known town or city of
S. Cataldo in Sicily, which was dedicated to his
memory in 1607.

Cathaldus has been honoured with a liturgical
cult, at least since the second half of the eleventh
century. A special office in his honour was compiled
after the finding of his relics, and in 1580 this was
revised and, to the chagrin of many a pious Taren-
tine, several of the old miracles and legends were
omitted. Three feasts are mentioned, March 8, May
8, and May 10. The most universally celebrated one
and the one given in the Roman martyrology and
in the present Irish *Ordo*, is May 10, which is
generally considered to be the anniversary of the
finding of his remains. March 8, which was also his

7

feastday in the Irish *Ordo* until about 1914, is taken to be the date of his death, while May 8 is believed by some to be the anniversary of one of the transferences of his relics, and by others to be due to a scribal slip for March 8. Taranto celebrates three feasts, his birth on March 8, the finding of his body on May 10, and his patronage of the place on September 3. New offices for all those were compiled about the end of the last century. It has been suggested that the St. Cartault or Catas honoured at Seurre, at Sens, and at Auxerre in France is our Cathaldus in disguise.

Cathaldus is invoked against drought, tempests, epidemics, perils of land and sea, public calamities and personal ailments. In Malta and Lombardy he is invoked especially to cure or preserve from hernia. Since the fifteenth century, Roccaromana in the Campagna holds a special thanksgiving ceremony for its preservation from the various epidemics of plague and cholera that attacked the neighbouring towns. A biography published during World War II proclaims him on its title page as the special patron of the soldiers of Italy. The list of miracles attributed to his intercession is a lengthy one and includes cures of paralysis, epilepsy, insanity, blindness, purulent sores that would yield to no natural remedy, preservation from imminent danger of shipwreck and drowning. Taranto has a saying: *"S. Cataldo fa sette grazie ogni giorno"*, that is, "St. Cathaldus confers seven graces daily."

And now the question poses itself, who really was this man whose cult has been so lasting and so widespread? Alas! that was the part of my quest that proved most disappointing. Here is all that can be asserted about him with certainty or with a fair degree of probability. There is no question of an empty tomb or a figure of vapour. He is a real person who died during the second half of the seventh century, or possibly the first half of the eighth. He was buried with great honour in Taranto in the place where stands the baptistery of the present cathedral. If we can believe what we are told, namely, that when his body was exhumed in 1071, or as others would have it 1051 or 1095, it was clothed in pontifical garments, we can take it that he was a bishop. Certainly, the fine marble sarcophagus indicates that he was a personage of importance. Judging by the contemporary or near-contemporary account of the prodigies that occurred on the occasion of the re-discovery of his body in the twelfth century, we can conclude that this was probably the body of a saint whose virtues God willed to make known. The name of this saintly bishop was *Cathaldus*, and he seems to have been known as Cataldus or Cathaldus of Rachau or Rachua.

The late Father Felim Ó Briain, O.F.M., did not believe that Cathaldus was an Irishman, nor did J. F. Kenney, it seems, although he does not say so openly. Thomas Dempster, who appropriated so many saints for Scotland that he was nicknamed "The Saint-stealer", claimed, of course, inevitably that Cathaldus was a Scotsman, but it comes as more of a surprise to us to find the learned Bollandists in one of their modern publications doing the same. Nevertheless, I do not think we can be accused of rashness if we continue to believe that he was an Irishman. Though continuity was broken and race memories blurred by wars and devastation, it is quite conceivable that some waifs and strays of a genuine tradition about him survived in or about Taranto. Then, the name Cathaldus is patently but a Latin formation from the well-known Irish name Cathal. Rachau or Rachua, of which we shall speak again, also sounds Irish and probably embodies as its first element the Irish word *ráth*, "a circular fort". With the exception of a note in a later hand in the Martyrology of Donegal, his name does not occur in the Irish festologies, but the same fate has happened to other Irish saints who lived and died abroad. Nor do I see any difficulty in accepting the tradition that he was an Irishman returning from a pilgrimage to the Holy Land.

All the rest is surmise or imagination. We are told that he was born at Catandum in Munster, that he attended the school of Lismore and later taught there, that he performed many miracles, which caused an envious chieftain Meltridis to denounce him to the king and have him thrown into prison, that after the death of Meltridis the repentant king granted some of Meltridis's territory to Cathaldus, that he became bishop over this territory of Rachau and had twelve bishops under him, that he later set out for the Holy Land and settled down in Taranto on the way back. He is said to have evangelized this town, which had fallen back into the ways of paganism, but others go farther and say he was chosen as its bishop and that during his tenure of office he corrected abuses, reformed the liturgy, and built several churches.

Certain other details to be found in his biography must be treated with suspicion, though it is difficult either to prove or disprove them. Such are, that his father's name was Euchus or Euchadius, which would represent Irish Eochaidh, and that his mother was called Achlena or Athena, which probably stands for Irish Eithne; that a druid or wise man called Dichu prophesied a great future for him; and that he built a church dedicated to the Blessed Virgin Mary at Rachau.

But there are certain other variations of and accretions to his legend that should be rejected without scruple. He was not appointed bishop of Taranto by St. Peter. He was not ordained priest by St. Patrick. He was not a brother of St. Donatus a reputed bishop of Lecce. He was not the author of a book of homilies for the people nor of a book of visions. A prophecy attributed to him, which was alleged to have been discovered in 1492 in the church of St. Peter outside the walls of Taranto is certainly spurious. And it can be stated that nearly all the miracles attributed to him during his lifetime are but hagiographical commonplaces, borrowed from other saints' lives by some unscrupulous mediaeval scribes.

Cathaldus and the cause of historical truth continue to suffer from his biographers even down to our own day. Chafing under the restraint imposed by paucity of reliable material, they invest his career with details devoid of all foundation in the sources and frequently lacking even a semblance of truth to recommend them. An example is one of the most recent biographies in Italian. Not merely is the character of Cathaldus vividly delineated in it but that of his father and mother. His father was a fervent Christian, inflexible in his principles, of a frank and open disposition. His mother was pious, a mirror of virtue, charitable and modest. She was a woman of prayer, and the people of the district used to call her "The Saint". His parents' names were Henry Sambrak and Aclena or Kathleen Milar. They lived in their ancestral castle situated in the town of Rachau, called *Mons Fabae* by the Romans. The town was situated on the top of a hill at whose foot flowed the River Bride. It was twelve miles from the city of Lismore in Co. Limerick. Cathaldus was the first-born of his parents and luminous prodigies accompanied his birth. At the time that Patrick came to Ireland, Cathaldus was teaching in the university of Lismore, and when word reached him that Patrick had landed at Dublin, sixty miles from Lismore, Cathaldus found means of meeting him and was ordained priest by him.

What is our authority for the name Cathaldus? An excellent one! It is the name, but spelled without the *h*, inscribed on a plain gold benedictional cross found in the tomb that was exhumed at Taranto in the eleventh century. The experts assure us that it was written in the seventh or eighth century.

The chieftain Meltridis of one of the legends may be Moelochtrige, king of the Decies, who gave land at Lismore to St. Carthage, and who died in 645.

The name Rachau or Rachua is generally considered to be the place in Ireland of which Cathaldus was bishop, rather than his birthplace. The authority for the name is the gold cross already mentioned, the first two letters occurring immediately after the name Cathaldus and the rest continued down the vertical beam. The same experts believe it was written in the eleventh or twelfth century, but I should not be surprised if it is seventh century. The writing is obscure. According to some it is *Famulus Christi*, "Servant of Christ", but most people read Rachau. Dr. Pentland Mahaffy, who examined it about 1888, also read Rachau and accepted it as a reference to an otherwise unknown Irish ecclesiastical foundation. Some, taking the *u* as an error for *n*, identify the place with Rathan, now Shanrahan near Clogheen, Co. Tipperary, where there are remains of an old church and monastery. My own reading is Rachua, Irish *Ráth-Chua*, and I have seen reference to an old fort of the name near Shanrahan. The neighbouring mountain range used to be known as Sliabh Cua.

The name Catandum given in the old liturgical office as his birthplace has been identified by some with Canty, near Lismore, by others with one of the two Ballycahills in Co. Tipperary. My own guess here is that an Italian biographer, remembering the mediaeval custom of calling a man away from home by his birthplace, surmised his native place was Cathaldum, which became corrupted to Catandum.

The cult of Cathaldus followed a development parallel with the discovery and transference of his relics. About 1071, when the cathedral was being rebuilt, workmen excitedly summoned Archbishop Drogo to a fine marble sarcophagus they had unearthed, from which emanated a delightful, fragrant odour. It contained, we are told, the body of a man clothed in pontifical garments and the name Cathaldus was inscribed on the gold cross on his breast. Several miraculous cures took place. In 1107, Archbishop Rainaldo ordered a re-examination of the remains and had them placed in an urn at the foot of the high altar. In 1151 Archbishop Giraldo caused them to be placed in a new silver urn and to be transferred to a special chapel on the epistle side. In 1339 Archbishop Ruggiero Capitignano placed them in a precious reliquary and had a bust of the saint made from the silver urn. Examination of the urn revealed that the tongue was still fresh and incorrupt. In 1465 the statue was made into a full figure. In 1737, during repairs, the skull and other relics were discovered wrapped in a silken bag within the head of the statue. The skull was placed in a special reliquary. The statue was remade in 1804 and again about 1891.

My visit to Taranto may not have thrown much further light on the problem of the historical Cathaldus, but from the point of view of learning about his cult and legend it was a rewarding experience. There is nothing to disprove that Cathaldus, like Columbanus and Gall, was not one of that noble band of Irish monks who helped to sustain a falling world. His cult is another reminder of the vast influence for good exercised by Irish monks from Ghent to Taranto, from Angouleme eastwards to Vienna. To many men it has been given to bring forth good fruit during their lifetime. Whatever work of evangelization and reformation of manners Cathaldus brought about in life was trivial in comparison with the amount he has since accomplished.

Over a wide area of southern Europe his strong hand has been the stay and support of peoples tottering on the abyss of disbelief and neo-paganism, not merely in the seventh but also in the twelfth, the sixteenth, the nineteenth, and the twentieth centuries.

VIII

THE ACHIEVEMENTS OF OUR

IRISH MONKS

BY REV. PROFESSOR JOHN RYAN, S.J.

M. DANIEL-ROPS, of the French Academy, a scholar known to all the world, called the book on the Irish monks, which he edited a year ago, *The Irish Miracle.* It is a title which he would find it easy to defend. In the broad sense of the word the miracle is obvious; what our Irish missionaries achieved was an object of wonder. In the stricter sense of the word again the term miracle is justified, for our Irish missionaries could not have achieved what they did without the special grace and favour of Almighty God. If the achievement is marvellous, the marvel lies essentially in the supernatural order; the merely human powers of man could not of themselves produce it.

You will think, perhaps, first of all, of the extent of territory which our Irish missionaries traversed.

In the world of to-day, where every capital city is, as it were, round the corner, the distances covered may not seem great but to contemporaries who knew the problems of travel they would appear very impressive. Modern parallels might be, perhaps, journeys to the Eskimo settlements in the Arctic, to the Russo-Chinese borderland, to the jungles of central Africa. The one and only purpose of all this journeying was, of course, to preach the Gospel message. "Go, teach all nations . . ." By the will of its Divine Founder the Christian religion is Catholic; it is meant for all mankind. "As the Father hath sent me, so also I send you," Our Lord said to the apostles. That was the beginning of the Christian mission. The apostles in their turn sent others to preach, and the process continued and will continue as long as even one nation remains outside the Christian fold. There is the mission *par excellence,* that to peoples still in paganism. There is the mission to people who were once part of the flock but who wandered from it along paths of heresy. There is the mission to people who are Christian indeed but who have no priests, no Mass, therefore no sacraments, like the first Catholic colonists in Australia, and to people whose clergy are so few or so inactive that the spark of faith in their midst is all but extinguished.

In each of these ways our Irish missionaries were active. Let us glance at their work in Scotland. There the most celebrated name in the story of conversion was that of St. Colmcille. He is rightly revered as the Apostle of Scotland. At his death so much of Scotland was Christian that his successors in Iona were able to complete the work. Of course St. Colmcille's personal contribution was largely organization; his primary duties lay within his own monastery, wherein he was abbot. He had responsibility, too, for the other monasteries, like Derry and Durrow, of his congregation. Nor should we forget the friends from other parts of Ireland who were but too anxious to assist in the labour of evangelization. St. Comgall of Bangor and St. Canice of Aghaboe accompanied St. Colmcille to the fortress of the Pictish king near Inverness, in the first great effort to win the good-will, or at least the neutrality, of that ruler. St. Comgall and St. Colmcille both had foundations on the island of Tiree, near Iona. St. Brendan of Clonfert seems to have made missionary journeys, short or long, to Perthshire and beyond. So, too, St. Bairre or Findbarr of Cork, and two saints named Faelan, one of whom is mentioned in the opening lines of Scott's "Lady of the Lake".

> Harp of the north, that mouldering long hast hung
> On the witch-elm that shades St. Fillan's spring.

And there are yet others, St. Ronan, St. Molua, St. Flannan, who gave his name to the Flannan Islands, some 30 miles west of the Hebrides. St. Donnan of Eigg, with no less than 52 of his community suffered martyrdom at the hands of pirates, no doubt from Norway or Denmark, in 617. You can picture to yourselves those zealous servants of God, the Irish monks, at Melrose by the Tweed, at Ardrossan on the Firth of Clyde, along the winding lochs and lonely haunted islands of the western sea, and inland over that broad expanse of petrified billows, carved by the twin artists, ice and water, which form the highland mountain chain. In a word, the epoch-making event in the history of Christian Scotland was the coming of St. Colmcille to Iona. The Irish monks converted Scotland to Christianity. As a consequence the Church in Scotland was an offshoot of the Church in Ireland to such an extent that from the sixth to the eleventh centuries—the days of St. Margaret—Irish influence on the development of the Church in Scotland was simply overwhelming.

I have dwelt so long on the evangelization of Scotland because it is there that the Irish monks first showed their capacity as missionaries. From Scotland, as you have heard in the lecture on St. Aidan of Lindisfarne, went forth the Irish missionaries who were to convert to the faith more than half of what is now England. The little island of Lindisfarne was to become in the words of the celebrated Englishman, Alcuin, *"locus cunctis in Britannia venerabilior"*, the holiest place in all England. From Lindisfarne, still known as "Holy island" Christian life was to radiate over all the Northumbrian realm; later, too, over the great midland region of England; and ultimately to the territory of the East Saxons—Norfolk and Suffolk—and even to the southern kingdom of Wessex. St. Aidan himself will live forever in the pages of the Venerable Bede. Indeed that author can hardly find words in which to express his admiration of Aidan's character—the gentleness, the piety, the ascetic moderation, the absolute other-worldliness, the boundless devotion to the needs of his flock. As Bede says, St. Aidan's person was a powerful recommendation of his teaching. A liberal supply of helpers, imbued with a like spirit, was sent to him from Iona. After 16 years as bishop and missionary he was taken ill near Bamborough, and there on the bare ground, his back supported by the wooden buttress of the little church or oratory, in a poverty and detachment worthy of his Divine Master, he gave back his soul to God. But the work of conversion went on. Many of the young English converts came to Ireland for their studies and in their turn became inspired by the missionary ideal. "O memorable time" (I quote Cardinal Newman) "when St. Aidan and the Irish monks went up to Lindisfarne and Melrose and taught the Saxon youth and when a St. Cuthbert and a St. Eata repaid their charitable toil! O blessed days of peace and confidence when the Celtic Maeldub penetrated to Malmesbury in the south, which has inherited his name, and founded there the famous school which gave birth to the great St. Aldhelm. O precious seal and testimony of Gospel unity when, as Aldhelm in turn tells us, the English went to Ireland 'numerous as bees'; when the Saxon St. Egbert and St. Willibrord, preachers to the heathen Frisians, made the voyage to Ireland to prepare themselves for their work; and when from Ireland went forth to Germany the two noble Ewalds, Saxons also, to earn the crown of martyrdom. Such a period, indeed, so rich in grace, in peace, in love, could last only for a season."

A distinguished English scholar, Dr. Lightfoot, did not hesitate to write that St. Aidan held the first place in the conversion of his race. To use his own phrase: Augustine was the apostle of Kent; Aidan was the apostle of England. It is true that the mission sent under Augustine by St. Gregory the Great made small progress for a long time and that from the day of St. Aidan's arrival in Northumbria the work of conversion proceeded apace until all England was Christian. To St. Augustine and his missionaries at Canterbury their due honour. In the conversion of England our Irish missionaries shared success with Pope St. Gregory the Great and that, for each one of them, would be an unmerited distinction and the highest reward.

As St. Colmcille and St. Comgall were intimate friends it is obvious that the story of missionary success in Scotland was well known in Bangor. We may take it then as probable that St. Columban was influenced by the example of St. Colmcille.

You have heard that in St. Columban's day work for souls on the Continent might take one or other of three forms: (1) work for those who professed the Catholic Faith but whose lives were grossly out of harmony with their professions; (2) work among schismatics; and (3) work among the pagan tribes. St. Columban applied himself to all three. There is no need to repeat the wildness and indeed the savagery of conduct which was normal everywhere in Merovingian Gaul. The Burgundians near St. Columban's monasteries of Annegray, Luxeuil and Fontaines were certainly not behind the rest in deeds of violence and bloodshed. St. Columban's presence in their midst brought about a mild (perhaps not so mild) transformation. People crowded to Luxeuil to do penance and in due course to receive the sacrament of reconciliation. The very sight of the self-denying life led by Columban and his monks was an encouragement to better ways. After his expulsion from Burgundy, St. Columban settled in Lombardy where the majority of the people were Arian heretics and many of the Catholics were divided from the Apostolic See by schism. He laboured manfully to bring these back to the Catholic Faith. It was a happy thought of Mademoiselle Dubois to mention St. Columban as a possible patron for the present oecumenical movement. As the separation of Christians, one from another, and their hostility one to another, filled his great soul with sorrow, as he spared neither pen nor voice in his efforts to bring back to the one visible flock, the Body of Christ, those who had wandered from it, so those who to-day labour in the same noble cause, in circumstances which the sins and faults of former centuries have painfully aggravated, can look to St. Columban for heavenly sympathy and help. Columban before the foundation of Bobbio spent some time preaching the gospel to pagan tribes in Switzerland. This work passed to his disciple, St. Gall, whose cell was surrounded by the pagan Alemanni. St. Columban was anxious to penetrate still further into heathen territory, to the lands of the Veneti, but was warned by an angel, his biographer relates, that God's Providence called him elsewhere. But the pagans of eastern Europe were never far from his thoughts. When his successor as abbot of Luxeuil visited him at Bobbio—a delightful reunion—Eusthasius received orders to send a missionary expedition to the pagan Warasqui.

St. Columban would not thank us if we spoke

so much of him that we neglected to speak of the other Irish saints in Gaul. We might mention St. Cillian, near Arras, and St. Fiachra. The latter's tomb became a place of pilgrimage, whence the cars used to carry the pilgrims to and from the holy body came to be known as *fiacres,* a term that survived into our own times. Fridolin of Poitiers was regarded by his biographer as an Irishman. He founded the important monastery of Säckingen on the Rhine and his cult became widespread in Switzerland, Germany and Austria. An Irishman named Tomméne was bishop of Augoulême in the decade 667–677. St. Fursa who was a missionary in Suffolk left England for Gaul. At his death his body was borne by the mayor of the Palace in Neustria to a new church nearing completion at Péronne. The body remained in an incorrupt state and soon became an object of veneration. Fursa's brother was Faelán and the two had been together in England. Faelán and his monks crossed over to Gaul and settled beside Fursa's tomb. Later he moved north to Belgium. There, at a place called Nivelles, the widow, Ita, and the daughter, Gertrude, of Pippin the Elder, had founded a convent under an Irish Rule. Ita was the first abbess. She died in 652. Gertrude, the second abbess, died on St. Patrick's Day, 659, assisted on her deathbed by the priest-monk, Faelán, just mentioned. Naturally he pointed out to her the happy augury: St. Patrick and hosts of angels would be waiting to give her soul a fitting welcome to its heavenly home. Faelán finally founded a monastery at Fosses, near Namur. Having lost his way in the neighbourhood he was murdered by a robber-band, under circumstances dramatically reconstructed by the Bollandist scholar, Père Paul Grosjean. Faelán was succeeded at Péronne by his brother, Ultan, who in his turn was succeeded by another Irishman named Cellán. He died in 702. An inscription in verse, composed by him for a chapel dedicated to St. Patrick, survives from his pen. Under 779, the *Annals of Ulster* record the death of Móinán mac Cormaic "Abbot of Fursa's monastery in France". Other references suggest that Péronne remained an Irish foundation—Perrona Scottorum—until destroyed by the Vikings about the year 880. From all this you will realize the good name which Ireland enjoyed abroad. In this connection a curious incident, political however, not religious, may be recorded. It belongs to the year 656. The King of Austrasia, Dagobert III, had just died. This was the period when the kings were figureheads and real power was exercised by the Mayors of the Palace. Sigibert's Mayor, Grimoald, son of Pippin the Elder of Landen, had the Merovingian heir, Dagobert II, arrested, forcibly tonsured and sent to Poitiers for shipment to Ireland. Why to Poitiers? No doubt because of the age-old wine trade. What Dagobert thought of this country is nowhere related. This is indeed a pity, for he stayed here about twenty years. He was called home in 676 but three years later was murdered. Pippin of Landen, you will recall, was the founder of the new Carolingian dynasty, made famous forever by the brilliance of Charlemagne.

In what is now south-western Germany Christians were fewer in numbers and much feebler than in

Gaul. It was thus a field for missionary work. Over a large area—Franconia, Thuringia, Alemannia, Suabia, Bavaria (which then included much of what is now Austria)—the main work of conversion was done by Irish missionaries or by local disciples whom they trained. While this historical fact is certain, little detail can be given, since records either were never made or were made but have not survived. The names that emerge are few. At Würzburg the fame of St. Kilian lives on. He was martyred there, with two companions, by the local pagans. In one of the lectures of the present series you have heard of St. Vergil of Salzburg. In a sense, he carried Ireland with him to that lovely city, famed to-day not only for its scenery but for its music. Vergil was abbot of the monastery of St. Peter in Salzburg, and as abbot administered the diocese for many years without receiving the episcopal order. Functions which lay beyond his powers as a priest were performed for him by an episcopal colleague, an Irishman called Dubdácrích. Later Vergil was consecrated bishop himself, but there must have been a time when Salzburg looked like a fraction of Ireland transported to Austria. For in Ireland during that century the abbot of the great monastery was the person who represented ecclesiastical power as distinct from ecclesiastical dignity. In the hierarchy of order the bishop was admittedly far superior to any abbot, however mighty and famous, who was merely a priest.

Before we pass from these German peoples it must be added that in quite recent times some new facts have come to light. A book by a Czech professor of archaeology was published in Prague in 1958. It contained the results of excavations made a few years back on sites that proved to be ecclesiastical. The remains of three ancient churches were found. In type they were neither Roman nor Byzantine, but in construction like those known to have been used abroad by the Irish missionaries of the seventh and eighth centuries. What is the likely explanation? All this is Slav country. Now the Slavs further east on the Danube, when attacked by the Avars in 745, had appealed to the Bavarians for help. With the military aid went a priest from Salzburg, a priest indeed from that very monastery of St. Peter's over which the Irish St. Vergil ruled as abbot. Later Charlemagne himself drove the Avars out of Moravia. By 796 their power was at an end. Bavaria and Moravia had now a common frontier. Missionaries either of Irish race or under Irish influence entered Moravia, built these churches in the style to which they were accustomed, and set about converting the heathen Moravians to Christianity. The dates tally perfectly, for archaeological evidence of itself is sufficient to show that the churches were built about 800. In other words Irish missionary influence was felt in this Slav country some seventy years before the coming of the two native saints, Cyril and Methodius, revered as the Apostles of Moravia. It would appear then that the work done by St. Vergil was on a scale even beyond what we had till now known; that missionaries formed in his school, not the less important because they remain anonymous, crossed the frontier between Bavaria and Moravia and were active in the latter area long before the coming of Saints Cyril and Methodius. This is not to detract from the fame of the two apostles, whose work was of a high order and lasting, but it does add something to the history of Moravia to recognize the merits of those who laboured there towards the end of the eighth century.

What is most surprising of all is the existence of Irish missionaries in Italy. We think of the two great apostles, Peter and Paul, preaching the faith of Christ in Rome, Peter with vivid memories of the Last Supper, of Calvary, of the first Easter morn, of the Ascension, and Paul with his relatively recent and tremendous experience on the way to Damascus. That the Irish, whose own conversion was to belong to the fifth century, could have helped in part to establish, in part to correct, in part to intensify, Christian life in the Italian peninsula is remarkable once again to the point of marvel. Yet we have St. Columban in Bobbio in the north and St. Cataldus in Tarentum in the south, and no doubt many others whose names may remain perhaps forever hidden, but may again one day be made clear from a complete and critical study of the documents.

Dealing with missionaries the stress has of necessity been laid on their activities as such, that is to say, on their preaching of the Christian Faith and Christian morality. Nevertheless it would be wrong, in dealing with our Irish missionaries, to omit all mention of their contribution to the well-being of the Church in the intellectual sphere. To take one outstanding example: a whole lecture might be devoted to the intellectual culture of St. Columban. He could see nothing wrong in combining this with religion. By the date of his birth the Irish monasteries were normally schools of knowledge as well as schools of religious observance. To the passion for the life of perfection was added a singular thirst for knowledge. Perhaps this is to put the matter in false perspective: it might be more correct to say, to the Irish mind true knowledge was a most valuable aid to holy living. To love God surely one must begin by knowing God. And the argument might continue: the fuller the knowledge of God, the greater the love of God in the heart should be. Bangor, at any rate, had a first-class school. St. Columban profited by his studies there. Though he was a very busy man he found time to do some writing. We have from his pen a monastic Rule and a Penitential and six letters (all dashed off to meet urgent problems and one, at least, of very great length), a few powerful sermons and finally—surprising in a man of his stern character—a number of poems, including a boat-song for use on the Rhine. What is truly amazing is his grasp of the Latin language, the ease with which he handles it as a medium of expression. He had that *recti generis voluntas,* the sharp sense of style, which Quinctilian regarded as the hall-mark of the truly educated man. Now such an interest in education was a veritable godsend to Merovingian Gaul, where standards had become barbarous; and to northern Italy, where the invasion of the Langobards was at that moment threatening to bring all civilization to ruin. Look once again at his work. It is a fact of history that he brought a breath of new Christian life into Gaul, Switzerland and Italy. Through his influence no less than fifty monasteries were founded. In all these the Columban, or rather the Irish, concept of learning would be cherished. If Luxeuil was famous for fecundity, no less famous were St. Gall and Bobbio as homes of piety, learning, Christian culture. And what holds for St. Columban holds, in its degree, for every one of the other Irish missionaries. It is not by accident that St. Vergil of Salzburg defended two theses that caused scandal to the ignorant of his day, the two theses being the sphericity of the earth and the existence of Antipodes. Immense indeed was the culture which these men of Irish race brought in dark and troubled times to a large area of Europe, the most important continent in the world.

From Inverness, then, to the Serbian border, from the North Sea to the Adriatic, the voice of our Irish missionaries resounded. What Scotland, England, Holland, Belgium, France, Germany, Austria, Switzerland, Italy, owe to their unselfish labours will not be known until the Judgment Day. They supplied that wide area for about two centuries with a superabundance of religious life. They tapped the fountain of grace, which flowed in living streams over whole countrysides, giving the soil a rich fertility that it never has quite lost. And when, in God's Providence, a similar need was felt, no longer merely in Europe, but in whole continents, in the nineteenth and twentieth centuries, the example of these old missionaries was felt as an inspiration to the young, boys and girls, to journey abroad as priests and brothers and nuns and teachers and medical helpers, to continue the divine work of bringing souls to the feet of Christ and to peace and rest in heaven.